The ABC of foster-family care for children - Primary Source Edition

Paget, Blanche J., 1874-1965, Pennsylvania. Bureau of Child Welfare, Anonymous

UNITED STATES DEPARTMENT OF LABOR

FRANCES PERKINS, Secretary

CHILDREN'S BUREAU - - - Katharine F. Lenroot, Chief

THE ABC

of

FOSTER-FAMILY CARE
FOR CHILDREN

Bureau Publication
No. 216

UNITED STATES

GOVERNMENT PRINTING OFFICE

WASHINGTON : 1936

•

CONTENTS

———

LETTER OF TRANSMITTAL

U. S. DEPARTMENT OF LABOR,
CHILDREN'S BUREAU,
Washington, February 15, 1936

MADAM. The A B C of Foster-Family Care for Children, first issued by the Children's Bureau in 1933, is now reissued with revised suggestions for further reading. The pamphlet was originally published in 1929 by the bureau of children of the Pennsylvania Department of Welfare, which acknowledged the assistance of the child-welfare division of the Public Charities Association of Pennsylvania in assembling a State-wide committee to sponsor the project and in securing Blanche J. Paget to write the bulletin.

In the introduction to the bulletin as originally issued, the late J. Prentice Murphy, then executive secretary of the Children's Bureau of Philadelphia and chairman of the sponsoring committee, said that the "handbook is intended for the use of all who receive for care children who can not remain with their own families, and as a special aid to those engaged in placing children in foster-family homes Many institutions do more or less of such placement; all of them receive children under the same conditions as do child-placing agencies. It is hoped that this outline of principles and practice may prove useful to officials of children's homes, poor-law officials, and others who place children incidentally, as well as to the representatives of child-placing societies The aim has been to adapt it to the needs of agencies depending wholly or in part on untrained and volunteer service."

The fact that the use of foster homes as a method of caring for dependent children who must be removed from their homes greatly increased during the depression made the publication of this bulletin by the Children's Bureau especially timely Its publication by the Bureau with such minor changes as were necessary to adapt it for Nation-wide use was approved by the author, the Department of Welfare, and the Public Charities Association of Pennsylvania. A continuing demand has caused the present reissue.

Respectfully submitted.

KATHARINE F. LENROOT, *Chief.*

Hon FRANCIS PERKINS,
Secretary of Labor

THE A B C OF FOSTER-FAMILY CARE FOR CHILDREN

FUNDAMENTALS

LABELS

The law classifies children who come under its protection. One whose family can not support him or who has lost his family is "dependent." If his parents willfully fail to provide for him or treat him cruelly, he is "neglected." If in response to a bad situation he rebels or breaks some law, he is "delinquent" In reality these classifications are vague and overlapping. As definitions they are both inaccurate and dangerous. Labels have a way of sticking, and if there is one thing that needs emphasis more than another it is that situations and persons are too complex to be readily explained or precisely classified. There is a common impression that the majority of dependent children are orphans, but at present the full orphan is rare in social work. The foundling with no known relatives is equally unusual, and cases of abandonment by parents of children not already in the care of some agency are not common. Parents so immoral or incompetent that they should under no circumstances care for their children are the exception. Nor would the unmarried mother swell very largely the number of dependent children if she could always obtain adequate support for her child without parting with him.

An inspection of applications made to almost any children's agency would show a number of children who must be provided for temporarily, and a few for whom provision must be permanent because of the physical or mental disability of parents. Many applications would be the result of poverty, usually complicated by sickness and unemployment. A surprising number would be the direct or indirect outcome of the separation of parents or of the desertion of one parent.

KEEP THE CHILD IN HIS HOME

Child-welfare work should begin with the assumption that the home is the basis of the social fabric and the right and natural setting for any child. Efforts to aid children which ignore this are unsound and are not true expressions of child-welfare work. The preservation of the child's own home should be the first aim. It is better to prevent an orphan than to care for one. Efforts to prolong life through improvement of health and prevention of accidents are more fundamental than the provision of insurance benefits or public assistance, such as aid to children deprived of parental care. The recognition that any reasonably good mother is the best and most

1

economical caretaker of her children marks an immense advance over the orphanage.

Among the problems that still press for solution are better marriage laws, education for parenthood, and other measures tending to increase the stability of family life   On the economic side efforts to lessen unemployment, to raise the level of wages, and to improve living conditions must be recognized as more vital to the children of the future than any amount of provision for the care of children away from their own homes

For the children of the present the first lines of defense are the family or children's agency, which maintains the home, the mental-health clinic, which helps to adjust the child in his home; the hospital, which returns the worker to his job; the special agencies and the courts, which straighten out conduct difficulties in the home

The child-placing agency should see itself in the light of a reserve to be called upon when all else fails.   Separation of a child from his family should be a last resort   But if families are not to be broken up unnecessarily, there must be close working relationships between child-caring agencies and the public and private organizations which aim to protect the home from disaster   The condition so often found where more funds are available for child care than for help to the home must be met and overcome.   The mother who hesitates to accept relief to enable her to keep her home together must be educated to see that it is far more self-respecting to do so than to be willing to part with her children.   Agencies must learn to recognize those qualities which, even in a poor home, may transcend any artificial substitute.

WHEN FOSTER CARE IS REQUIRED

In spite of every effort to preserve the home a certain number of children must be cared for away from their own families.   Once it was deemed enough if these unfortunates were kept alive and saved from the worst forms of suffering   Now people are beginning to see that true child welfare means the provision, for every such child, of those things which his own home should have given him.

Let us make that abstraction, the " dependent child," concrete by imagining that by some not incredible freak of fortune he is your child or mine, and then ask ourselves what is the least we should demand for him.   That " least " which he would need is just what every child needs, as much for the good of society as for that of the individual concerned   It is true that in many families which should be kept intact not all those advantages which are every child's right can be secured for the children, but these lacks may be overbalanced by certain intangible spiritual qualities to be found only in a child's own home   When children must be deprived of these values certainly those minimum essentials which every child should have should be sought for them in whatever homes are substituted for their own.

WHAT EVERY CHILD SHOULD HAVE

1. *Security.*—A feeling of stability, and of belonging and counting for something in other lives.

2. *Family life.*—A chance to live in a normal family group of differing ages without being crushed by numbers; to develop mutual attachments and a sense of responsibility for others and for the work of running a household.

3 *Sufficient nutritious food.*—This should be simple, well prepared, and adapted to the age of the child. It should be served at regular hours, amid attractive surroundings, and eaten at leisure in a cheerful atmosphere.

4. *Adequate shelter.*—A clean, light, well-ventilated, well-kept home, properly heated in winter, with sanitary toilet facilities. The child should have a separate bed and a place in which to keep private possessions and to entertain friends.

5. *Comfortable clothing.*—Clean, whole, attractive garments that fit and that are individually owned; sufficient changes for cleanliness; adequate protection against inclement weather.

6. *Health habits.*—Individual toilet articles; frequent baths; proper care of teeth; regular bedtime and plenty of sleep, abundance of fresh air and of pure drinking water; several hours of outdoor play each day; definite teaching of health rules and of wholesome, happy, courageous attitudes; sensible instruction in sex matters.

7. *Educational essentials.*—Attendance at a community school of good standards as long as the law requires, and as much longer as the child's capacities warrant. Development of each child's fullest capacities through high-school, commercial, or trade-school training in line with special abilities.

8 *Recreation*—A safe, clean, roomy place for outdoor and indoor play; suitable play material and tools; sympathetic supervision.

9 *Community life.*—A part in community group activities and festivities, opportunity to make friends in natural ways through entertaining and being entertained; normal neighborhood contacts and wholesome association with persons of the opposite sex

10. *Moral and religious training*—Positive teaching of standards of right and wrong aside from measures of discipline; daily contact with adults of sound character and inspiring personality; attendance at religious services of the type preferred for each individual case

To give these things to every child received under care may seem like a large order. But the task is simple compared to dealing with the adult incompetency and delinquency which result in a large number of cases from failure to do so. It is not too much to say that the child-caring group which is unable to assure these character and health building essentials to the children it receives into its care had better withdraw from the field or limit its activities to fewer children.

FIRST STEPS

WHO SHOULD SIFT THE APPLICATIONS

The interviewing of applicants should be done by one of the most experienced and capable individuals connected with the organization, not, as is often the case, by the least competent person. A first interview should be somewhat like the preliminary examination of a good physician It should be light and gentle and only thorough enough to determine whether the seeker has come into the right hands or needs the services of another sort of specialist. If it becomes clear that some other organization can help the family best, the questioning should end, but there should be no careless and hasty shifting of responsibility   To send a poor mother trudging from place to place in search of aid is cruel, and it is also a waste of valuable time for all concerned

The decision as to whether a child needs to be removed from his own home should be made by someone with broad experience and training in dealing with social problems. Organized volunteer groups or public-welfare boards providing services for children but having no specialized staff should not undertake the care of children away from their own homes unless the groups are affiliated with a State or county department or a well-organized private agency that can provide expert assistance and consultation on case problems. With expanding programs of State and local public services for children, such assistance should be possible even in small communities If an agency has no qualified staff, a committee headed by the member of the board who combines with human sympathy and insight the widest knowledge of modern methods of child welfare will be found of great help in deciding on the reception of children.   She should build up a group of persons willing to give time and thought to each individual problem as it arises, until such time as it is possible to secure trained service.

Responsibility for the care of a child is a serious business, not to be assumed lightly or carelessly   The place to avoid mistakes is at the start   It is easier to keep a home together than to reconstruct it Temporary care to tide over a supposed crisis is too apt to prove permanent; the emergency becomes chronic, as maladies have a way of doing when not properly treated   For an agency to accept a child merely because some one asks it to is as illogical and as likely to lead to bad results as if a physician were to let a patient make his own diagnosis and prescribe for himself.   Were a major operation involved, this would be regarded as criminal   Removing a child from his home is a major operation.   Only those should undertake it who are better qualified to judge the need than is the suffering family. The decision should rest, not on what the applicants say they need, but on what the facts show.

Each application must be judged on its own merits, but experience has shown that there are certain typical situations in which foster care is unnecessary and even harmful   In certain other situations, such care is almost inevitable.

CHILDREN WHO SHOULD NOT BE REMOVED FROM THEIR HOMES

1. *Children eligible for long-time public assistance or entitled to insurance benefits.*—Public assistance or insurance that will make it possible to keep children in their own homes should always be drawn upon before private funds are used.   The groups of dependent children eligible for long-time care from public funds vary in different States.   The legislation in a number of States, however, conforms with the requirements of the Social Security Act, which includes any dependent child deprived of parental support or care by

reason of death, continued absence from the home, or physical or mental incapacity of a parent, and who is living with his father, mother, grandparent, brother, sister, stepparent, uncle, or aunt.

2. *Children who are fatherless or motherless and for whom only temporary care may be needed* should be provided for in their own homes whenever possible. In many cases financial assistance will enable a mother to carry on alone. The father who has the entire responsibility for the care of the children, even though his income is fair, is frequently in need of assistance in financing and arranging for housekeeping service. A few of the more progressive agencies have recognized the desirability of providing housekeeping service rather than removing children during the temporary absence of the mother. Courts, public welfare officials, and private agencies must be brought to accept the principle that no child should be separated from his parents or from a surviving parent because of poverty alone.

3. *Children whose fathers are abusive or will not support them* but who have good mothers should be protected by court action. The punishment should fall on the offending fathers. If a home is broken up, it is the mother and children who suffer.

4 *Children of parents who wish to separate but who give their children good care.*—Such parents should not be encouraged to separate by an agency's easy acceptance of the children Many a tottering home would be preserved if the parents could find no way of escaping their joint responsibilities.

5. *Children of divorced parents, one of whom wishes to remarry —* Children are quite frequently placed with the frank admission that a present or prospective stepparent objects to their presence in the home. These parents should find that society does not countenance such easy shirking of parental duties.

6 *Children whose relatives can care for them* too often are accepted by an agency without due inquiry into family circumstances.

For children born out of wedlock no rules can be laid down except the general one that, with encouragement and help, mother love often triumphs over great obstacles; that nothing should be done in haste and without knowledge of all the facts; and that lack of support should never be allowed to separate mother and child.

CHILDREN WHO NEED FOSTER CARE

1. *Orphans* with no relatives able to care for them

2. *Foundlings* with no known relatives.

3. *Children abandoned* by parents who are known but can not be traced.

4. *Children who have no parents in the home able to give care.*— When neither parent is able, because of illness or incapacity, to maintain a home, it is necessary to provide care for the children. Tuberculosis and mental trouble frequently cause this situation Whenever there is hope of reconstructing the home, care should be taken to emphasize the temporary nature of the separation.

5. *Children removed from unfit homes by court action* —These children must usually pass into the care of some organization, but their acceptance involves an obligation to see that everything possible is done to fit the home for their return.

6 *Children born out of wedlock* —Physical or mental unfitness of the mother to care for her child, extreme youth of the mother, and various other factors may warrant separation.

7. *Children with certain serious health problems* are sometimes benefited by a period of foster care in a favorable environment. This is true particularly of pretuberculous children and heart cases

8. *Children presenting special mental, conduct, or habit problems with which their parents have proved unable to deal.*—Many such children are being successfully treated in carefully chosen foster homes. Treatment should be accompanied by careful study of each individual case.

WHAT MUST BE KNOWN BEFORE DECISIONS ARE MADE

Even when applications are rejected or referred elsewhere, the following information is necessary for identification and should be filed for future reference·

1. Date of application.
2. Surname of child, with cross reference in cases of later marriages of parents.
3. First names of parents, maiden name of mother, ages of parents. their color, religion, marital status (single, married, widowed, or divorced).
4. Addresses of parents.
5. Names of children in order of age, birth dates, whereabouts if not with parents. Check names of children for whom care has been requested.

This is enough to identify the family. More is needed to serve as a basis for intelligent judgment, as, for instance—

6 Occupation and approximate earnings of wage earners in the family, especially when poverty is pleaded.
7. Other persons in the household and their contribution.
8. Reason for requesting care and length of time the trouble has existed
9 If there is illness or physical disability, what medical care has been given.
10. What help the family has already had.
11. What near relatives there are, including married children
12. What relatives, if any, have helped or have been asked to help.

NECESSARY COOPERATION

Before any action is taken inquiry regarding the family should be made at the social-service exchange, if there is one Where a number of agencies are functioning in different centers, an exchange organized on a county basis is practical. In its absence every agency or individual at all likely to be helping the family in question should be consulted People who do this for the first time are often amazed at what they learn. The facts may be quite other than they are represented. Some one may be carrying out on behalf of the family a careful plan which would be destroyed by placing the children Or an organization which should be helping but has lagged may be spurred to immediate action by knowledge that the parents are trying to place the children. If others are trying to aid the family any plan entered upon by the children's agency should be a joint one.

If the family should be kept together, but does need help, the first thought must be for such immediate aid as may be necessary to tide them over until a plan can be formulated. A family-welfare society, churches, fraternal organizations, and clubs are the most likely sources of emergency relief In making a permanent arrangement for the family all existing types of public assistance, including insurance benefits, should be utilized first. If funds from these sources are unavailable or inadequate to meet the need, private sources of help should be sought. Relief should be regular and adequate, and the plan should provide for aid to be given without repeated solicitation as long as the need continues. Health needs should receive immediate attention To give aid to individuals whose condition demands medical care without making sure that they get it is to pour money into a sieve.

Unfortunately there is often a gap between theory and practice In many communities public assistance is still inadequate or poorly organized In such places there is likely to be no organized family relief agency or, if there is one, its funds may be used only for emergency aid. Churches, fraternal societies, and clubs are difficult to hold to a sustained program. If the trouble seems to be health, there may be a hospital, clinic, or visiting nurse to meet the need— or there may not be. The children's agency or the institution has received popular support and has long borne the brunt of family misfortunes. The weight of public opinion and support is unfortunately often in favor of its continuing to do so, in spite of the social and financial cost involved in the needless breaking up of families.

The interested organizations can arrange for concerted action on such family situations through case conferences of their representatives. Such a group might undertake also to work for more adequate relief funds. Even when no other help seems at hand for a family, it may be the duty of the enlightened children's agency resolutely to refuse admission to children who should remain at home, even though it must itself provide the relief needed to keep the home together. Later, perhaps other sources of relief can be developed.

Tell the parents your decision. "Have you come for the children? I been keepin' 'em home from school all week thinkin' you might come any day," said Mrs. Green to the agency visitor. No parent need ever be left in such suspense. If no help seems to be needed, this should be explained. If another organization is being asked to visit, the family should know what to expect. If it seems probable that the children must be accepted, make no premature promises but let the family understand that it will be necessary to consult some references, see the children, and learn all about them in order to know just what they need and to plan for them wisely.

THE INQUIRY

MORE THAN AN INTERVIEW NEEDED

More than a single interview is needed on which to decide, even temporarily, the destiny of a child. In dealing with human lives one has no right to act blindly. It is a duty to find out as much as possible: First, to make sure that there is no possibility of keeping the child with his own people. In the second place, the child must be known if his deeper needs are to be met. Thirdly, the facts about him should be recorded. The child has the right, as an individual rooted in the past, to have these facts preserved for the use of those caring for him and for his own later knowledge.

WHO SHOULD MAKE THE INQUIRY

This depends on local conditions. An adequately equipped children's agency with experienced paid workers always prefers to make its own inquiry. If the staff of the agency is limited or no paid workers are employed, assistance in making investigations may be obtained in some communities from social workers of other agencies. This help might come from the case worker of a family-welfare agency or from the case worker of a public welfare department or of the juvenile court. When the board members of the children's agency must undertake the investigation, every effort should be made to do this as thoroughly as would a professional worker.

Whoever makes the inquiry should have a reverence for family ties and the knowledge that nothing has yet been discovered comparable to the family as a place for the nurture of children. The apparent urgency of the particular situation, the difficulties of local conditions, and the problems involved in the kind and length of care needed are but surface factors and must not be allowed to cause panic and sudden decisions nor to hide the graver issues involved. Situations are rarely so urgent that children need be received into care before the facts listed in the following section are known.

WHAT FACTS ARE NEEDED

1. *The family history* leading up to the crisis which prompted the request for care.

2. *The antecedents and early life of parents*—their ancestry, childhood, chances for education, their hardships, work life, and other items.

3. *The financial circumstances* of the family in detail—wages of working members, property, savings, insurance, rent, and general scale of expenditure, so that the need can be gauged accurately.

4. *The standards of living* and the care given children must be seen at first hand in the home.

5. *The character of the neighborhood* should be noticed.

6. *Church and Sunday-school attendance* of children and of parents, the name of the church and of the pastor.

7. *Personal history of the child.* Children have all had individual experiences which have helped to mold them. Even small things may have great significance.

8. *School record* and opinion of teacher, mention of special abilities and disabilities, interests, and companionship.

9. *Health history* of the child and his family. The presence of infectious disease and the present physical and mental condition of the child.

10. *Near relatives*—their names, addresses, and circumstances, their willingness and ability to help, ascertained through visits when possible.

11. *Legal points*, which should be verified:

Birth dates of children (through the division of vital statistics of the State department of health, through local registrars of vital statistics, or through baptismal certificates, church records, or other reliable sources).

Marriage of parents (through marriage certificate, court record in county in which marriage took place, or pastor's statement).

Death of parents (through the division of vital statistics of the State department of health or through the local registrar).

Legal settlement of family.

WHERE AND HOW TO GET THE FACTS

Social agencies should be willing to share the information which they possess, just as physicians do when they consult about the best treatment for a patient. Consultation with other organizations knowing a family should precede any extended inquiry. This will save much time, useless questioning, and the following of false leads.

The applicant (usually the parent) should be encouraged to talk freely by a sympathetic listener. Most parents approach the threshold of a welfare agency with heavy hearts and have suffered acutely before reaching the point at which they are ready to part with their children. Some come with a defensive attitude or a ready-made story which they soon forget if they feel that they have found a real friend. Others, and they are often the best, find it anything but easy to tell their troubles to a stranger. If the initial facts seem to show a real need for care, there may be no more propitious time for a satisfactory talk than at the moment of the request The conference should be unhurried, the questioning tactful, the interview private. It is especially unwise to have children present, a fact which mothers seldom realize.

The child who is to be taken under care is the person most concerned. If he is old enough to realize what is in the wind, he is old enough to have feelings and opinions about the situation, and he should be given a chance to express them. At least, some explanation is due him before he is transplanted to a strange environment. The cheerful side of things should be stressed to him, and high tragedy should be avoided.

Relatives and references—In visiting references it is well to keep in mind that the quality of the interviews counts far more than the number of persons seen. A friendly smile and a frank, businesslike explanation quickly win confidence. The agency visitor should go not as a spy but as a friend of the family, with an air of leisure but with a clear idea of what information is wanted. One can get the opinion of the person he is seeing without expressing his own. The visitor need not doubt his right to ask questions, but he can ask them considerately, with an open mind and an impartial attitude. A visit to one relative may give a complete picture of the family, but if it is necessary to see ten, the welfare of one child is worth the trouble.

Care should be taken in seeing neighbors, but neighbors who are intelligent and kindly disposed may prove a valuable source of information, suggestion, and aid, especially in small towns and rural communities.

Physicians, ministers, lawyers, and teachers who know the family are all valuable sources of information. Employers may prove helpful, but it is well to be cautious about seeing present employers lest the fact that aid has been suggested create a prejudice against the employee

The inquiry should be entirely matter-of-fact and aboveboard. There should be nothing surreptitious about it. The family should be told that references must be consulted   Except where deception has been practiced or there is evidence of neglect and abuse of the children, any wishes expressed by the family should be respected. Great care should be taken not to violate confidences nor to stir up trouble. No promises should be made, or even implied, which can not be fulfilled.

WHAT MUST BE RECORDED

Recording accurately the information obtained, while it is still fresh in mind, is quite as important as gathering it. Human memory is prone to error, and the personnel of agencies constantly changes. The future welfare of the children and the protection of the agency itself demand that all pertinent facts be set down as clearly and completely as possible. It is better to record something irrelevant than to miss something that may prove highly important later. For purposes of accuracy it is well to take down names, addresses, and dates during the interview, though it should be done unobtrusively so as not to distract attention. The distinction between proved facts and mere impressions should be clear. The source of all information should be given.

WHAT SHOULD BE DONE NEXT

When all the facts that can be learned are at hand a social diagnosis of the trouble should be made and the best treatment decided upon. If the care needed seems to be more than temporary or there is any possible alternative to foster care, it is far wiser to have a group consider the case. If the family has been under the care of other organizations, their representatives should of course be brought into this conference or their opinions obtained beforehand

A tentative plan, put down in black and white, stating the apparent needs of the child and the family, what remedy is proposed, and the final end in view, is wonderfully helpful and clarifying.

THE FOSTER HOME

THE LEAST THAT SHOULD BE EXPECTED

1. *A dependable income* sufficient to provide a comfortable living.
2. *Housing* that provides light, heat, ventilation, sanitation, and adequate room for the family.
3. *Home-making*—cleanliness, order, proper preparation of food, and homelike surroundings.

4. *Health*—all members of the household free from communicable disease or any defect that could affect a child adversely

5. *Neighborhood*—healthful with satisfactory sanitary conditions and outdoor play space. Good neighborhood influences for older children Home near church and school and reasonably accessible.

6. *Education and intelligence*—no stated amount of education required, but native intelligence and good sense vital.

7. *Moral standards*—uprightness in business and personal relations imperative. Dependability in living up to agreements and reliability in carrying out directions.

8. *Religious training*—participation in church activities as well as church attendance desirable. A favorable attitude toward religious training for the child in accordance with the faith of his parents is essential.

9. *Atmosphere*—foster parents sympathetic, cheerful, and able to understand child nature and needs; harmonious in their own relations; successful with their own children, if they have any

10. *Motive* for taking a child should be acceptable to the agency; it should not be self-interest.

TYPES OF FOSTER HOMES

There are four well-defined kinds of foster-family care; namely, boarding homes, free homes, adoption homes, and wage homes. *In the boarding home* the foster parents are paid for their services—and by service is meant not merely food and shelter, but such personal care and training as a child should receive in his own home. *In the free home* exactly the same care is given without money compensation to the foster parents *An adoption home* is a free home accepted with the understanding that if the situation proves satisfactory the child will be adopted. In case of adoption the foster parents assume all the legal and social obligations and privileges of actual parents *In the wage home* the child is on the same footing as in the free home; that is, he should be a member of the family, not a servant, although he is paid for definite work performed; under changed industrial and social conditions it has become increasingly difficult to find this type of home.

For children in boarding, free, and wage homes the placing agency, whether or not legal custody has been given, stands in the position of guardian and protector of the child and retains the privilege of supervision and removal. After the completion of adoption proceedings, the agency no longer has any such privileges.

THE BOARDING HOME

Advantages.

More extended use should be made of boarding homes. In some localities there is a tendency to regard the foster parents who accept pay for their services as grasping and actuated solely by money considerations. The fear that the children may be exploited is a wholesome one, but in the case of the properly safeguarded boarding home it is quite as ungrounded as in that of the carefully selected free home. Food, shelter, and oversight are bought as a matter of course for children in institutions, and one never thinks of the members of the staff as " mercenary " because they are paid. Nor does anyone

suppose for an instant that the paid social worker is any less conse-
crated to her task than the volunteer

The contribution made by foster parents of the right sort far out-
weighs any money compensation, but so far as money can reward them
they are as fairly entitled to a wage as a visitor or the executive of
an agency. In fact, while the agency may guide, it is the foster
parents who pull the load. The time is past to depend wholly on
the home that can volunteer its services.

Where the boarding home has fallen into discredit it has done
so because of careless and inexpert selection, poor supervision, too
low a rate of board, and failure to protect the foster family and
child through good medical service. The compensated private home
is capable of absorbing a number of children once thought unplace-
able. This is not to say that the free home need be ruled out Many
children and even certain types of handicapped children are being
successfully treated in free homes by agencies of high type. But
the sphere of the boarding home can be greatly enlarged with profit
to all concerned, especially for certain types of children who in the
past have suffered from unwise placements in free homes. The
agency ready to pay adequately for necessary care has a greater
range of choice in its selection of homes, is less limited as to the types
of children it can serve, and is altogether more flexible than the
agency wholly dependent upon free homes.

Children for whom board should be paid.

1. *Very young children,* whether they are later to be returned
to their own people or to be permanently placed. A foster mother
can scarcely be expected to spend her strength without compensation
on a child whom she must finally give up, but children should not be
taken permanently by foster parents until it is quite certain that
development will be normal. The best home for a baby is not always
best as the child grows older. A woman who makes an excellent
nurse may not be able to cope with older children. The baby home
should be exceptional from the standpoint of health, and it should
have a quiet, kindly atmosphere, but such factors as education and
neighborhood influences are less important than for an older child.
The effect of the temporary foster home on the baby's parents may
need to be considered, especially in the case of unmarried mothers.

2. *Motherless children whose father should retain control and
responsibility.*—Even if a father can not personally care for his children, he should not relinquish his rights and responsibilities and let
someone else support them.

3 *Children whose history indicates possible physical or mental
defect.*—Letting foster families regard such children as their own
has often led to heartbreaking disappointments. Such children
should remain unconscious of their status, but it should be clear to
the foster parents, and too close identification with the family
should be avoided

4. *Children with obvious physical or mental defects.*—Cripples
and children who have heart affections, who are predisposed to
tuberculosis, or who have venereal infections need a kind of care
which should be well compensated. Very young children who are
deaf, blind, epileptic, or high-grade feeble-minded may be far better

off in a private home than in an institution until they are old enough to benefit by institutional care.

5. *Normal children who present special conduct or habit problems* —These are usually the older children, but the selection of a wage home, too generally used for this group, is a great mistake for any child whose troublesome habits more than offset any service he can render. The bed wetter, the child who offers a sex problem, who has temper tantrums, or who has formed the habit of petty theft or of running away should be regarded as a patient to be cured before being expected to hold his own in the world. He needs even more intelligent and painstaking treatment than the child who is physically ill. Problem children should be kept busy, but their work should be part of the process of fitting them for a useful, normal life. The foster parents who are to succeed with them must have unusual insight, patience, and skill; but such homes are by no means so uncommon as might be supposed. They can be found, just as nurses can be found who are able and willing to tackle any physical problem, no matter how hard or repulsive it may seem; but such expert service must usually be paid for.

6. *Children who need temporary care.*—There are some real emergencies in which instant care must be given temporarily, but these are extremely rare. (See p 15)

Where to get the money.

The first thought should be of parents who for their own good should be held to their responsibilities to just the extent that they are able to meet them. This should not be a matter of guesswork but should be based on a careful study of the facts. When public resources are available they should be utilized in all proper cases. Dependent children usually are recognized as a proper charge on the public treasury. Private funds may be used to supplement inadequate public aid and to care for any case for which public aid can not be obtained.

How much should be paid? This will vary with the locality. The board for children must be graded according to the difficulties of the case, and rates for emergency care or short-time care should be higher than those for long periods. Even a high rate may prove a great economy in the long run.

THE FREE HOME AND THE ADOPTION HOME

Quality of the home.

The status of the child in a free home should be that of an own child. People who receive no money compensation inevitably expect a return in control of and affection from the child. The free home, therefore, becomes a preliminary to adoption or a relationship similar to adoption but lacking legal sanction because of the age of the child, possible claim by some relative, or some other element of uncertainty.

Safeguards should be thrown around children in free homes to prevent overwork, failure to be treated as a member of the family, and interference by relatives.

It is best that children in free homes be wards of the agency placing them.

The adoption home should be far more than " good enough." It holds the fate of a child   It should measure above the minimum that may be accepted in homes providing only temporary care.   The agency must in time withdraw its protection, so the foster parents must be intelligent and responsible enough to carry on without oversight.   The home should fit the child, not offering something beyond his capacities, yet representing the best to which he can reach, with surroundings under which he can grow to advantage   The spiritual qualities of the home are more important than mere material advantages.   Children for adoption should be drawn from the same groups as for free-home placement, but with added restrictions to be detailed later.   (This subject is more fully treated in the section on adoption. See p. 34)

Children for whom placement in adoption homes is questionable.

1. *Foundlings*—When nothing is known as to the child's heritage, neither adoption nor free placement should be considered until the child has been examined for possible physical or mental abnormalities.   (See p 36)

2. *Abandoned children.*—Much is often learned as to the background of abandoned children, hence the risk is not so great as in the case of foundlings   Free placement, if the child is normal, is sometimes preferable to adoption, however, because of the possibility of future claims on the part of relatives.

3. *Children removed from unfit parents by court action* should not be rushed into free homes   The parents should have every possible chance before their final separation from the children is effected   If the separation does become final, it should then be complete.

4. *Children whose parents are both incapacitated permanently* (an insane mother and a crippled father would constitute such a situation) and who are without relatives to care for them can be cared for in free homes.   Anything so final as adoption is not usually advisable.

5. *Orphans* may be placed in adoption homes or, if they are unsuitable for adoption, free homes may be best for them.

THE WAGE HOME

Except when the work is used as vacation occupation for older children who are still in school, the wage home should represent an opportunity for training and the acquisition of real skill   Domestic service for the girl and farm work for the boy may be nothing but " blind-alley " jobs.   On the other hand, they may provide preparation for life or the beginning of a career.   This depends on what kind of home is chosen and how it fits the aptitudes of the particular child.   Wage homes should be selected with quite as much care as those for younger children.

The arrangements with foster parents should be businesslike—it is well to have a written agreement—but the child's welfare and happiness should take precedence over mere support, and the agency should maintain the same friendly concern and supervision as in other forms of placement.   Children placed in wage homes should have reached the limit of what school can do for them.   They should be strong, capable, and old enough to do what is expected of them without injury.

Requiring children to earn all or the greater part of their maintenance while still in school in order to obtain higher education is a practice that calls for many safeguards. Generally it should be discouraged for children under 16 years of age or before entrance into high school. Even with older children, unless both foster home and child are exceptional, harm or failure may result

On the other hand, it is very desirable even in free or boarding homes that children should be given a chance early in life to earn money at useful tasks suited to their strength. This money should pass through the child's own hands in order that he may learn its value. It should be applied to something more tangible and satisfying to him than reduction of the amount paid for board. He should be taught how to save and how to spend wisely for useful and cultural things. Foster parents, of course, should not be expected to pay a child for his share of the routine household chores such as would be performed as a matter of course by their own children. They should try to offer special tasks which the child may perform of his own free will in order to earn something.

TEMPORARY CARE

WHAT IS AN EMERGENCY?

Numerous receiving homes are maintained throughout the country by foster-care societies, juvenile courts, and county and other agencies. Most of them were established for the excellent purpose of keeping children out of almshouses and jails. Yet many are not much better than the things they replace "But what shall we do in an emergency?" exclaimed the perplexed board member when her proposal to open a "temporary shelter" was blocked by the very person who had been vigorously protesting against sending children to the almshouse.

Real emergencies requiring immediate removal of the children are extremely rare. In most cases in which this is done the children concerned would suffer less harm if left in the situation in which they were found, or with kindly neighbors, until all the facts could be learned and a plan formulated Then it frequently will be found that they need not be taken at all. Family situations often need first aid on the spot, but seldom the clanging ambulance and the emergency ward Inexperienced workers are easily panic-stricken and do not stop long enough to find out whether the supposed crisis is not in reality either a chronic or a superficial condition.

It is easy to destroy family life. During the influenza epidemic, while a young mother lay desperately ill, her husband died Assuming that she also would die, relatives broke up her home, scattered her possessions, and rushed her little children to an institution She got well, but it was many years before she was able to reestablish her home, and the children suffered irreparably. Had her children been with her, she would have been eligible for mothers' aid

The agency that receives children before making an inquiry faces great disadvantages. It is much harder to secure information from the family, since they can not see the point of answering questions after the event. Relatives in a position to give good care are less likely to be willing to take a child already in responsible hands. Children received without preliminary study and physical examination may prove to be serious problems requiring a type of care other than the agency is prepared to give, or they may be suffering from some infectious or other disease which should have been treated first.

CHILDREN WHO MAY NEED TEMPORARY CARE

1. Children who must be cared for pending investigation.
2. Children awaiting a court hearing or decision.
3. Children for whom a permanent home has not yet been found.
4. Children needing study and special training before they are placed permanently
5. Children needing special medical treatment not involving hospital care.
6. Children taken only for a short time to tide over a real crisis, such as temporary illness of their mother.

WHY NOT USE FOSTER HOMES FOR TEMPORARY CARE?

The boarding home is being used successfully for short-term care in many places The foster family is infinitely preferable to the almshouse or jail, and it has been found practical to substitute it even for the juvenile detention home caring for supposedly difficult children It has many advantages over congregate care

Not the least of these is the *lessened danger of infection.* Not only is there less mingling of children when they are distributed in private homes, but also a case of measles or whooping cough endangers only the few children who happen to be in the same home. Quarantines of all children in care are avoided, obviating the expense of holding for long periods children otherwise ready for discharge and the inconvenience of being unable to accept children who need care

Through the foster-home method, families of both sexes and varying ages, who must otherwise be separated, may be cared for together The danger of contact with children who have had unfortunate experiences or acquired harmful habits will be obviated. Children uprooted by a family upheaval will suffer less through placement in a kindly family than through the new and often terrifying experience of a stay in a receiving home with many strange children.

Temporary care in foster families is practical So far it has been developed most fully by city agencies which have highly efficient methods of family care and a group of experienced foster parents. In small centers in which resources are few but neighborly feeling is strong, the boarding home is by far the best way to solve the problem of emergency care. There, one or two homes, chosen for their adaptability and kindly atmosphere, should fill the need.

The foster parents who give temporary care should be able to win children quickly and make them feel at home; yet they must have a light touch, keeping the relationship casual and free from over-attachment The management of a changing succession of children, with a minimum of friction and maximum health results, is an expert's job, yet it is possible to find foster parents who take satisfaction in doing it for that very reason. It is work of high value and should be well compensated. Rates of board for emergency or short-time care should be higher than for long periods. If necessary, the foster parents should be assured of a minimum income whether there are children in the home or not; that is, the home should be subsidized. Homes used for temporary care should contain no young children and should conform in all respects to the qualifications for foster homes. (See p. 10.)

Foster care is best for babies. The individual attention that can be assured only in a private home is essential for babies Under the best conditions they often tend to thrive but poorly under congregate care. From the standpoint of economy also, the private home is better for the very young child

In the temporary placement of babies, as for longer care, any State requirements in regard to licensing should be rigidly obeyed. One child, or, at the most, two children, are enough for a baby home The income from boarding a baby should be welcome but not essential to the family. The chief motive should be genuine love for little children, an unselfish love that is content to give with no hope of the return of affection that would come if the child could remain.

As a solution for the unmarried mother and her child during the nursing period the temporary boarding home is sometimes the best choice. If the mother is reasonably competent and is free from infectious disease, she should be encouraged to keep her child. To further this and to maintain the physical welfare of the baby, the mother should nurse him if possible. If her own family can not be persuaded to receive her after she leaves the hospital or maternity home, mere lack of means may force her to part with her child. Even when assured of a meager income from the father for the child's support she may not know where to turn Boarding care for both in the home of a broad-minded, motherly woman during the period of adjustment is then most likely to lead to a satisfactory solution In other cases, or after the nursing period, it may be best to board the child apart from the mother for a time, letting her see him frequently and holding her responsible for his support. In a surprising number of instances this leads to eventual acceptance of the child by the mother and her family Needless to say, the influence of the foster family upon the mother is of paramount importance. Particular care should be exercised as to the men with whom she will be brought in contact by the placement.

FINDING THE FOSTER HOME

GETTING ON THE TRAIL

Breaking ground in a new locality in which people have not learned to regard the foster care of children as an honorable calling may require patience and persistence. The following methods of attracting good homes have been successfully used ·

Appeals to church and club groups.—Stories of foster care from the experience of other agencies may be effective here. Appeals should not be made for homes for particular children, as they are likely to prove embarrassing, since the applicant who most readily responds to the concrete appeal may be the least suitable. Names of children should never be given out

Enlistment of influential individuals such as physicians, clergymen, teachers. public officials, and selected laymen to speak to people of their acquaintance who might make good foster parents.

Advertisements in newspapers, farm papers, and religious publications are often quite effective   The following advertisement inserted in a Philadelphia newspaper brought 360 replies, about 15 per cent of which were promising material

> THREE little children, 4, 7, and 9 years of age, want to borrow a mother while their own mother goes to the hospital for an operation Must be Protestant; good neighborhood   Board $7 a week. References exchanged

Other foster families will be the source of some of the best homes coming to the attention of an agency. A few foster homes of high type in good neighborhoods will in time bring applications from neighbors and friends of like quality

General publicity—Anything which helps to make the work of the agency favorably known may draw foster-home applications. In all publicity the use of names, addresses, and identifying information about children should be avoided, as this is stigmatizing and demoralizing to its subjects and detracts from the dignity and trustworthiness of the agency using it   In fact, it should be considered a violation of confidence.

The best publicity, in the long run, is good, sound work. Poor work, on the other hand, will offset any amount of publicity and will soon make it difficult for an agency to secure reputable homes.

WHAT MUST BE KNOWN ABOUT THE FOSTER HOME

1. *Financial status of family*—approximate earnings, rent or ownership of home, probable savings

2. *Make-up of family*—the age, sex, occupation, and health of each member of the family and others in the household.

3. *Housing conditions*—the number of rooms in the home, the amount of sleeping room, sanitary conveniences, kind of furnishings.

4 *Housekeeping and home-making standards.*

5 *Background of foster parents* and as much of their history as possible.

6. *Intelligence of foster parents*—native intelligence, general information

7 *Education* and attitude toward school.

8. *Moral and ethical standards*

9. *Church membership* and attendance

10. *Interests*, social connections and diversions, community activities.

11 *Neighborhood influences*, including the type of community, school facilities, and children in neighborhood.

12 *Temperamental qualities of foster parents and others in household*—any friction in the home or strain in the atmosphere, the foster parents' understanding of children and ideas as to their management; their success with their own children; their general outlook on life.

13. *Reasons for taking a child*—financial; desire for companionship; desire to be of service; or other reasons.

14. *Reaction of foster parents* to explanation of the aims of the agency and the control to be exercised over the child.

HOW TO GO ABOUT THE INQUIRY

Use of social-service exchange.—In places having a social-service exchange it has become customary to inquire regarding foster families in order to learn whether or not some other foster-care agency already has known and used them. It is sometimes discovered that the family in question is known to a number of health and welfare agencies because it has received assistance from them, and these agencies often give valuable information. Of course foster parents are giving rather than receiving social service, and they may be and should be among the finest people in the community. That their names are entered in the index of a social-service exchange is simply a proof that inclusion in such an index is no reflection upon anyone.

If the application consists of a letter from the family containing very little information, it is well to send an application blank to be filled out. These blanks have distinct limitations, but they at least indicate the make-up of the family and may bring forth a few valuable references. If the applicant lives at a distance, letters to these references may well be the next move. If the replies are favorable, a visit to the home is next in order.

The first visit to the home—This should be made at a favorable time of day when the foster mother is likely to be at leisure. The interview should not consist of a series of questions but should be a friendly conversation that will put the applicant at her ease and allow her to reveal her real qualities. Before the end of the call the visitor probably will be invited to see the house. If not, this should be suggested.

The more that can be learned about the background and antecedents of the foster parents, the better. Every member of the household should be touched upon in the course of the conversation and, if possible, seen during the visit. It is extremely important, though often difficult, for the foster father to be seen before a home is used.

In seeking information about such matters as financial stability, the visitor must keep before herself and the foster family the thought that it is not only the right but the duty of the society to know fully about a home before placing a child in it. Courtesy and the implication of this underlying purpose will rob so-called "personal questions" of their offense. Of course the visitor must be able to inspire confidence in her discretion.

The visitor must have a clear idea of what she wants to know and must be keenly observant without being overcritical. She must have an eye for essentials as distinguished from the superficial. She should be absolutely noncommittal as to whether a child will be given to the family but should give a lucid explanation of the purposes and requirements of the agency. If it becomes clear early in the visit that the home is not desirable, the visit need not be prolonged.

Seeing references.—Before any home is approved, not only should the references given by the family be interviewed, but two or three independent ones gathered in the course of conversation with the family or secured from other sources should be seen References from whom letters have been received will almost invariably give additional information, and they will express franker opinions in a personal interview. While doubts remain on any point the visitor should continue to seek more light until these are settled beyond question.

The second visit.—A second visit to the home before it is finally approved is of the utmost value. This may be made by appointment with the definite object of meeting the man of the house or other members of the family not previously seen. The strangeness having worn off, the visitor may be greeted almost like an old friend. Under these conditions the conversation becomes easy and natural, and the real nature of the household appears more clearly. This visit sometimes will bring out facts not previously revealed that will show the inadvisability of using the home. More often, unsuspected values are discovered. In any case a second visit is sure to add much to the understanding of the home and to appreciation of what type of service, if any, it can best render.

The decision.—Before a home is approved it is always well to have a second person review the information and the impressions gained and assist in making the decision. This person may be another member of the staff or a board member. If the home is being considered for a particular child, better known to someone else than to the person who has investigated the home, there should be a conference between the two to consider the needs of the child in conjunction with what the home has to offer. When a home is used for the first time, this is most important.

Recording the information.—It is quite as vital to record the facts about the foster home fully and accurately as to record those about the child and his family. A complete account should be kept of what is learned through the visits to the home and from each reference. The source of opinions about the family should be clearly indicated, and those of the persons interviewed should never be confused with the visitor's impressions.

The foster family should be promptly notified, when a decision has been reached, as to whether or not to expect children from the agency. In case of disapproval the grounds for not using the home often may be frankly stated. as when the home is badly situated or the agency has no child suitable for it.

Good home finding is the " ounce of prevention" from the lack of which incurable harm may result. No part of foster-family work calls for more skill and wisdom. The visitor should be keenly aware of the responsibility she carries. She must realize that carelessness or lack of intelligence on her part actually may involve issues of life or death.

PLACING THE CHILD IN THE FOSTER HOME

FIRST STEPS

Arrangements made with the child's own parents, not through the courts, should be clear and definite and preferably should be made in writing so as to avoid misunderstandings. Informal acceptance of children not entitled to public support has the advantage of encouraging friendly relations with the child's family   The direct payment of board to the agency insures frequent contact   There are many responsible parents able and willing to meet their share of the cost of care

Reception of children through the juvenile court or public-welfare officials is advisable when there is serious doubt that the parents can or will meet their obligations or when they should not retain custody of the children. However, money considerations should not be allowed to outweigh the social needs of the family. When the parents can not pay the full cost of care, it is customary in some places for the court to place a small order on the parents, the difference to be made up from public funds   But in many cases children should be received from the parents without a thought of collecting support from any public agency.

A court commitment gives legal custody of the child, and no child should be received for permanent care unless transfer of guardianship is approved by a State department of welfare or a court of proper jurisdiction. A copy of this commitment should be kept on file by the child-caring agency.

Placement of children outside the State necessitates the filing of a bond in many States. Care should be taken to make such placements only with the knowledge and approval of that department of the State which controls child-welfare activities.

Medical examination should always be made before the child is taken. If it long precedes actual placement, an inspection for communicable disease must be made on the day of reception.

Authority for minor operations and inoculations should be given in writing by the parents at the time the child is received, as a protection to both the child and the agency.

Mental studies before children are taken for any prolonged care would be ideal, but the services of psychologists and psychiatrists are not available in many places. To be of value such studies must be made by competent persons. However, in some States the State department has, through its mental-hygiene services, facilities available for such examinations; and these should be utilized for children whose mentality seems at all doubtful as shown by the facts of heredity, personality, and the school record   Children who show peculiarities of conduct or mental development after coming into care should be examined at the first opportunity.

EMERGENCY CARE

Children who must be taken before a permanent home is ready or who are not in condition to go to one when accepted must have care in a special home   This should provide for isolation if there are suspicious symptoms and for treatment in case of skin eruptions or other infectious conditions not requiring hospital care. A foster mother with nurse's training may sometimes be found who will undertake this work   The qualities needed in such a home have been discussed. (See p. 10.)   This is a suitable time for correction of physical defects, such as diseased tonsils; for improving the condition of undernourished children; and for training children in good habits. It is during this period that the child, torn from his family for the first time, may suffer acutely from homesickness. He needs special attention and diversion, and these can be found for him more easily in a well-chosen foster family than in an institution where his individual needs can not be given consideration.

CHOOSING THE HOME FOR THE CHILD

Choosing the foster home calls for the wisdom of a Solomon It is well to have more than one opinion as to the choice. The child, his background, and the foster home should all be known at first hand by those making the selection. It is well to begin with certain general requirements and, after they are fulfilled, to pass to more particular aspects.

The child's background.—Children should be placed in foster homes of their own religion—Protestant, Catholic, or Jewish. The foster parents should, when possible, have the same racial background that the child may feel more at home and be weaned less from his own people. The " ways " of the two families should be somewhat the same.

Children of the same family should be kept together whenever possible, or at least in the same neighborhood. The scattering of families is one of the greatest tragedies of foster care. The insistence on keeping brothers and sisters together should not be carried so far, however, as to result in harm rather than good.

The health needs of children must be one of the first considerations. The needs of the baby home have been discussed. (See p. 12.) The undernourished child should have especially good food, outdoor life, and restful surroundings. The physically defective child must have a home in which his wants will be understood and met, but in which he will not be set apart by his disability.

The child in need of habit training must have exceptionally wise treatment and often is unsuited for placement in a home with other children. Children who have harmful sex habits or who present special conduct difficulties ought not to be in a home with other children, especially those near their age or of the opposite sex. The possible influence of the foster child upon the children of the family and their influence upon him should never be overlooked.

The older child will find it hard to forget his own family and former associations and to fit into new surroundings. If he is from a poor home, he usually is happiest in a plain foster home not too different from his own. A studious, ambitious boy does not belong in a rough farm home where a stolid youth of backward mentality might fit perfectly A crude girl of coarse background may be wretched as a member of a cultured family, whereas a girl with wild propensities but high intelligence may find it the very thing she craves.

Educational needs.—Educational opportunities should be kept in mind in choosing the home, especially for the child who has a high intelligence quotient or some special ability. An elementary school of good standards and access to a high school are essential. The exceptional child should be placed in an exceptional home providing the cultural or artistic atmosphere which he needs.

Placing as a fine art —The nice adjustment between the foster family and the child is the fine art of child placement.

Mary, a plain little girl of 10, and a pretty baby sister were placed with a highly conscientious maiden lady who had small experience outside her own circle The baby at once captured the hearts of the family They tried to do their duty by the older sister, but her crude ways shocked them. They were unaware that they showed any partiality, but soon Mary began to lie and to steal trinkets from her foster mother's room. Reasoning, scolding, and punishment only made her worse. She was finally transferred to the home of a sweet, motherly woman of less education but more experience and tolerance This foster mother's sympathies were aroused by an explanation of Mary's difficulties and she took the child to her heart immediately, whereupon Mary's faults vanished as if by magic.

Avoid undue haste or delay. "Act in haste and repent at leisure" happens only too frequently in foster-home work. On the other hand, it must not be forgotten that "hope deferred maketh the heart sick." A child should not be left too long in a bad situation while just the right home is being found.

INTRODUCING THE CHILD TO THE FAMILY

A preliminary visit to the prospective home by the worker placing the child is an important step, especially if the home has been found by someone else. The family should in this way be prepared for the kind of child they are to receive The arrangement with the foster family should be absolutely clear cut. The control to be exercised by the agency, what is expected of the family, and the financial arrangements should be gone over in detail before the child goes to the home. It is well to embody the main points in a letter to the family, a copy of which is kept on file by the agency, but care should be taken not to place too much reliance on written agreements They can never take the place of personal relationships based on friendly understanding and complete confidence.

What information to give the family.—Foster parents with whom one can not be fairly frank about the child's failings and experiences are seldom the right sort to succeed with children. Not all the confidential information about the child's family need be divulged, but enough must be told to give a real understanding of the child and of the influences which have made him what he is It is seldom safe to place a boy who has the habit of appropriating other people's property, or a girl who has had sex experience, without informing the foster parents The facts should be told sympathetically and without too much detail or emphasis.

Take the child into your confidence. Tell the child what to expect and make him feel that he is a welcome addition to the family. Plan the meeting between the child and the family so that the circumstances will be natural and he will not feel that he is on exhibition. See that he is well dressed and makes his best appearance. Stay with him until the first strangeness wears off. He should always be accompanied to the home by a sympathetic person.

After the child is left in the home do not rush around the next day to pull up the plant and see if it is rooting, but keep in close touch. Do not be surprised if you are asked to take the child away at once On the other hand, foster parents may be all enthusiasm so long as the child remains on his best behavior When the strangeness wears off, the trouble may begin. In either case the visitor must keep her poise, let the foster parents tell their troubles without interruption,

and try to find out what is back of the child's conduct. The foster
parents must be helped to see that difficulties were to be expected and
should not be taken too seriously. The child may have old habits,
faulty training, homesickness to combat. He may resent the ways of
the home because they are strange to him.

As they gain experience foster parents will learn all this. Those
who are new at the task must have much explained to them. The
best contribution the visitor can make is a sense of proportion and
humor. A hearty laugh has relieved many a tense situation; only
the laugh must never be at the child's expense.

SUPERVISING THE CHILD IN THE FOSTER HOME

WHAT SUPERVISION INVOLVES

Visitors who know what they are about.—Some training and experience in the principles and methods of social case work are essential
to good work. Sound knowledge of child hygiene and diet is important. A degree of maturity, a good general education, teaching
ability, understanding of children, patience, tolerance, and a sense
of humor are all needed. For the interested volunteer with this
foundation but no training there are many ways of gaining knowledge and skill. Special courses offered at schools of social work and
institutes held at State conferences or by national agencies should
be attended when possible State departments concerned with child
welfare, the Child Welfare League of America, and the United
States Children's Bureau can advise as to methods of self-education

Limitation of volume of work—No visitor, however capable, can
give proper supervision to 100 or more children at a time The
number she can handle will depend on local conditions, on the types
of children in her care, and on the amount of other work expected of
her. It is safe to say that the visitor who is supervising babies,
children who present special problems, or children placed for short
periods can not do justice to as many as 50 children. Inaccessibility
of homes and long distances also will affect the number of children
she can look after well.

Naturally, when the visiting is done by volunteers who have
home duties as well, even fewer children should be assigned, the
exact number depending upon the amount of time the visitor can
give. However small the number of homes a volunteer undertakes
to visit, she should take entire charge of them. It is not desirable
to have several visitors going into a home in the same period of time,
and the fewest possible changes of visitors should be made

The frequency of visits should be governed by the needs of each
case, but it is safe to say that visits should not be less frequent than
every three months. These visits should be made just as often as
is necessary—daily or every few days in a crisis, weekly or monthly
under other circumstances. They should not be limited to occa-
sions when something has happened but should be timed to antic-
ipate and prevent trouble In country districts it is best to avoid the
use of homes so remote as to make visits difficult at any time and
impossible in winter.

Outside contacts with the child, such as shopping expeditions,
pleasure trips, and other outings, are desirable in order to give the

visitor a chance to observe the child away from the influence of the foster home and under conditions that will encourage confidences.

Correspondence with the foster parents, the child's own family, and with the older children themselves should be used to supplement visits. It should be constructive in its nature, every letter being planned to accomplish something. All letters received should be kept, also copies of all letters sent.

Responsibility for medical care—Division of responsibility for medical attention varies with the type of home For the child in the boarding home the expense and most of the planning for care must fall upon the agency. In free and adoption homes the foster parents should be encouraged to take the initiative, the visitor making such suggestions as may seem necessary. A doctor should be on call for sudden or minor illnesses. Foster parents giving free care will naturally prefer their own physician, although the visitor may suggest the names of reliable specialists when they are needed For boarding homes it is a good plan to prepare a list of doctors in various neighborhoods who will respond to a call from the agency or foster parent.

Periodic medical examinations should be given to all children by a competent physician at least once a year; once in six months is better. Infants and children of preschool age should be under the continuous supervision of physicians or of physicians and nurses. Teeth should be examined twice a year.[1]

School reports should be shown to the visitor. They should be supplemented by conferences between foster mother and teacher and the former's report of the way things are going. In some cases it may be well for the visitor to interview or correspond with teacher or principal, but this always should be done in such a way as not to injure the child's standing with teacher or pupils.

Planning for the child's future should be a dynamic process. An agency should not be content to give care without concern as to the final outcome but should constantly shape its treatment to meet the child's developing needs. Definite education and training should be given for work which will provide the fullest possible outlet to the child's abilities. Failure, as well as success, should be anticipated and met courageously. Children who need permanent care should be accepted for better or for worse. The agency which sends a child to a correctional institution as soon as he becomes troublesome is missing its greatest opportunity for service. The institution or agency which keeps a child when some other type of care would better meet his needs is equally remiss

Guidance of intercourse with the child's own family.—Except when the parents exercise an undesirable influence or when the parental relationship has been finally severed by court decree, every effort should be made to keep home ties strong and wholesome. Foster parents should be warned against criticism of members of the child's family and alienation of the child from them. It may not always be wise to permit the child to visit his family, but parents should be encouraged to visit their children, and the older boys and girls should write to their families. Maintaining

---

[1] See Standards for Physicians Conducting Conferences in Child Health Centers U S. Children's Bureau Publication No 154. Washington, 1926

contacts between the child and his family, though it involves difficulties, is an inevitable part of good foster-family care.

The frequency and nature of visits from relatives must not be allowed to interfere with the child's progress nor to become too great an annoyance to the foster family. On the other hand, the visitor must see that the natural rights and privileges of parents are not forgotten and must be vigilant in preventing conflicts over the child. Thorough understanding and frequent contact between visitor and parents is the best way to control the situation.

A running record of information gained in the course of caring for a child is just as important as preservation of the findings of the original inquiry, which should be recognized as never final nor fully accurate. The visitor who does not keep a chronological history for each child in her care, noting each important action taken and each development, is borrowing trouble for herself, for her successors, and eventually for the child himself. Too much is safer and in the end is far easier than not enough, but the aim should be to make this record both concise and explicit.

Each visitor, whether a paid worker or a volunteer, should make a written report of every visit or action taken. This should be dated and signed, with the name of the child at the top of each sheet. A loose-leaf record, written on one side of typewriter paper and fastened to the child's face-sheet in chronological order, is best for this purpose. It will be better still if a stenographer or some volunteer able to use a typewriter can be employed to copy the reports consecutively as they are turned in.

THE VISIT TO THE FOSTER HOME

The quality of visits counts more than mere number. The time of a visit should be chosen to suit the convenience of the foster mother. It is hopeless to expect a satisfactory conversation with a woman who is preparing a meal. The visitor must be a good listener. After the foster mother has had an opportunity to tell all that is on her mind, without interruption, she will be ready to answer questions and listen to suggestions. The points to be covered should be clear in the mind of the visitor, but she should seek information rather by a skillful direction of the conversation than by a definite list of questions. Not every point, of course, need be covered in any one visit, but everything about which there is the least doubt should be cleared up.

WHAT THE VISIT SHOULD REVEAL

1. *The health of the child* as shown by physical appearance and by the report of the foster mother.

2. *The appearance of the child* as to neatness and cleanliness of clothes and person.

3. *Diet*—just what the child is given to eat, meal hours, appetite.

4. *Sleeping arrangements*—whether the child sleeps in a room or a bed alone or, if someone rooms with him, who this is; the condition of the bedding; ventilation of the room at night.

5. *General condition of house* as to order, cleanliness, sanitation.

6. *Provisions for recreation*—toys, constructive materials, and tools; place to play.

7. *Work the child is expected to do*—its suitability for his age; its amount; whether he is paid for any part of it.

8. *Spending money*—what the child does with it. (Arrangement should be made for a small but regular allowance to older children from the parent, the agency, or the foster parents.)

9. *School and community*—what the foster mother and the child have to say about school progress; the child's participation in group pleasures and community activities; his popularity, attitude, and friends.

10. *Church and Sunday school*—regularity of attendance and interest.

11. *Conduct and methods of discipline.*—The child's habits and reactions to home and school A knowledge of the punishments used is as illuminating as the child's misdeeds.

12. *The child's relations with the foster family*—his reaction to different members of the family; the degree of understanding and affection shown

WHAT THE VISIT SHOULD ACCOMPLISH

The visitor merely by showing her interest in the foregoing points as occasion arises centers the attention of the foster parent upon such matters and stimulates their zeal. Factors which they have overlooked or about which they are not informed are brought to light Difficulties created by the child are discussed in the light of his past history. His actions can be related to his needs and how they are being met; he may have been meddlesome because he had not enough to do, or irritable because of food that disagreed with him. The recital of injudicious punishments gives an opportunity to suggest wiser expedients

The visitor should not be too ready with advice and suggestion but should be encouraging and appreciative of the good accomplished She should bring to the situation a detachment and breadth of view which will lift the foster parents above the petty vexations of their task and stimulate them with the sense of being engaged in work of great significance and far-reaching consequences

DIVISION OF RESPONSIBILITY

What to expect of the visitor—The visitor should never regard her job as one of inspection but rather as one of friendly cooperation. If she is qualified, her relation to the foster parents will naturally be somewhat that of an office supervisor toward members of her staff. If she is not competent, insistence on "rights" and "authority" will be futile. True, it is her business to see that the requirements necessary to the welfare of the children in her care are fully met by the foster parents, but she should actively aid them to understand and meet their obligations, especially when they are inexperienced In this it is well for her to keep a humble heart, for often she can learn as much from foster parents as she has to teach them.

To the child the visitor should be a wise friend whom he can depend upon to be fair She should be some one whose approval he wants to win rather than whose displeasure he fears Any strong, emotional attachment of the child for a visitor should be avoided.

The more she can keep in the background of his life the better. Her criticisms and suggestions should be made to foster parents privately, never to the child or in front of him. When differences are adjusted in her presence, the visitor should provide the right atmosphere for an understanding rather than sit in judgment. The child should feel free and be given opportunity to confide in her but should not find in her a partisan.

What to expect of the foster parents.—Foster parents are not servants; they are members of the staff and should be so regarded. Before the home is used, the foster parents should understand the agency's need to know every important incident affecting the child They should agree to acquaint the visitor with all that takes place in connection with him, to report any change in the make-up of the family or their situation, and not to take a child to board from any other source. If the home has been wisely selected, they can be depended upon to meet these obligations and those connected with the care of the child to the best of their ability. Their ability must not be taken for granted, but complete confidence and friendliness should exist between foster parents and visitor.

If the child has lost or been permanently separated from his parents, foster parents should take their place as fully as possible. If the child is to maintain relations with his family and perhaps return home at some future time, an uncle and aunt relationship with the foster parents should be encouraged. In either case the foster parents should assume, in the eyes of the community, the place of relatives identified with the interests of the child. No effort should be made either to conceal or to advertise his connection with the agency.

Foster parents should be intelligent enough to look after the school interests of the child and to confer with the teacher as to his progress, the visitor intervening only in cases of serious trouble. It is the foster parents who should train and discipline the child, not the visitor.

If there is reason to question the good faith of the foster parents, a few of the most trustworthy of the original references or other reliable persons in the community should be consulted under seal of confidence. Otherwise, once the home is approved, the visitor should not discuss the foster family with neighbors No good foster family is free from the possibility of criticism The visitor must not encourage gossip and mere faultfinding but she must be alert for anything coming from the child or others which may indicate serious failure of the home to safeguard the child's welfare, or to live up to the agreement with the agency.

REPLACEMENTS

If the original selection of homes is intelligent, the transfer of children will be reduced to a minimum The experienced visitor does not get unduly excited when a foster mother frantically telephones to ask that a child be removed immediately. If the first understanding was clear, the foster mother may be reminded that this can not be done but that due notice must be given. A visit should follow promptly, in which careful judgment and keen insight will be needed by the visitor Is the difficulty trivial and temporary due to inexperience on the part of the foster parents, to lack of previous training on the part of the child, to the strain of a new adjustment, or to mere misunderstanding? Even when the trouble seems to be more fundamental, it may adjust itself before a new home can be found for the child. The necessary interval before a change can be made has saved many a good placement from early disaster. Even when a placement seems to leave much to be desired, careful consideration should be given to any change lest it be "out of the frying pan into the fire." It is easy to cultivate in a high-strung, restless child an incessant desire for change and a tendency to escape anything in the least unpleasant by running away from it. It is equally easy for a sensitive child to suffer serious harm in a well-meaning home where he is not understood. The best way to escape from this dilemma is to exercise the utmost care in making the first placement.

Some of the things to consider in making a replacement.—The effect on the child of being uprooted just as he is beginning to feel settled—of feeling that he is not wanted and is homeless—should weigh in any replacement. The continuity of his school work also is important. When possible, changes should be made at the end of the school year When the affection between the child and members of a foster family is strong, it should not be lightly regarded. It may sometimes be better to leave a child in a home to which he has become attached, even though it has not all the qualities one would seek for him if he were being placed for the first time.

The inexperience of foster parents and visitors is the cause of too many replacements. The home may be good but may need skillful interpretation of the child and the reasons for his actions A family which is inexperienced with children and unacquainted with social conditions outside its immediate circle is likely to be shocked by superficial things, such as a child's lack of table manners or the uncouthness of his relatives. If the visitor is equally unfitted to evaluate these shortcomings, many unnecessary transfers will take place

Good reasons for replacement —The placement may have been temporary, and the child may be ready for permanent placement. A change in the circumstances of the foster family, such as sickness or the arrival of other relatives who crowd the home, may make a change imperative The development of some hereditary defect in the child may make special care advisable and permanent placement on a free or adoption basis most unwise. Failure to make proper physical gain, after the elimination of factors other than the care being given, is a valid reason for removing a child from a home.

The persistence of conduct or personality difficulties in the child after reasonable efforts to help and educate foster parents to an understanding of the trouble, usually means that the right conditions for that child have not been found. Certain children present such outstanding difficulties that it is impossible to secure the complete readjustment of the child through one placement. He may have to pass through several homes in the process, each making its own contribution to his development.

A child may outgrow a family in which he thrived and was happy when younger. To leave a child with high intelligence in an uneducated family that can not give him the things he craves may starve his mind and breed impudence and self-conceit. Some foster parents who are excellent with little children can not cope with the adolescent.

Future educational needs should be provided for in long-time placements; but if it becomes necessary to move a child in order to give him proper educational opportunities, this should be done.

Opportunities for employment may be lacking in a community when a child reaches the age to go to work. In some such cases the work life must take precedence over family life.

The failure of a foster family to cooperate effectively with the society after earnest efforts to bring about the right relations means that the family must be dropped. As the child's guardian, the agency can not shift to other shoulders the responsibility for failure to meet the child's needs. The discovery of a serious moral defect in some member of the foster family makes it the agency's duty to remove the child. Sex irregularities or dishonest dealings should not be tolerated.

BUILDING HEALTHY CHILDREN

" Is Mary well? She seems rather pale and thin," said the visitor. " Oh, she's never sick," replied the mother, " she's always looked that way. It's just natural to the family. All the children are like that." Mary's mother did not know what every one who gives foster care to children should know; namely, that healthy children do not just grow; they are dependent upon good food, fresh air, rest and sunshine, and medical attention to prevent disease and to correct defects.

THE DOCTOR'S PART

The examining physician should be a competent general practitioner or, better still, a child specialist. He should have a genuine love of children as well as skill. Adequate compensation for his services is as legitimate a charge on a child-caring agency as the executive's salary or food and clothing for the children.

The medical examination.—An accurate knowledge of the physical condition of the child before he is received for care is imperative. A negative bill of health, such as " Henry has never been sick in his life," is not enough. Dr. Horace H. Jenks, late chief of the Associated Medical Clinic maintained by a group of child-caring agencies in Philadelphia, gives the following description of what a general medical examination of a child should be. It is quoted at length in order to give those responsible for the foster care of children an opportunity to familiarize themselves with the procedure and thus be able to judge the thoroughness of an examination for themselves:

Plenty of time should be allowed for the general physical examination, especially for the first examination * * * It is often well to open the interview with the child by some casual remark as to his interests in play or school, or the ever-interesting subject of what he likes to eat * * * The weight and height are recorded. Then, beginning at his scalp, the child is examined from head to foot. He should be entirely undressed as the examination proceeds * * * The dryness of the hair, the presence or absence of any disease of the scalp, as ringworm or *Pediculosis capitis* (head lice), is noted. As a practical point, it should always be recorded in the history whether or not nits are present. The nose should be examined for the presence of any nasal discharge, obstruction, or deflected septum, the mouth for the condition of the teeth and gums, enlargement or disease of the tonsils, general shape and condition of the palate The neck is felt for the presence of enlarged lymph glands and for examination of the thyroid gland

The chest, of course, should be most carefully examined Not only should the lungs be examined for bronchitis or tuberculosis, but the amount of air entering should be roughly considered. It is astonishing how poorly many undernourished children breathe * * * These children may need deep-breathing exercises fully as much as extra milk. The heart must be studied with reference to its size and efficiency as much as for the detection of murmurs or leakage at the valves

The abdomen should be examined with the child lying down and relaxed Enlargement of liver or spleen or the presence of umbilical hernia should be noted

Boys should be examined for phimosis, undescended testicle, and hernia, older boys for varicocele Girls should be examined especially for the presence of any vaginal discharge, and girls who are to be admitted to institutions or to homes where there will be other girls should have vaginal smears * * *. Both sexes should be examined for signs of irritation or inflammation of the genital organs caused by masturbation Next, the child's posture is studied, the condition of the spine, shoulders, legs, ankles, arches of the feet, and general bearing or carriage being recorded.

The child is then dressed and returns for tests of eyesight and hearing In babies and young children the eardrums should be examined with the otoscope Eye and ear examinations in general are not detailed, but if any abnormality is detected, the child should be referred to a specialist for more thorough examination

It is advisable, although it is not always practicable, to secure a specimen of urine at the first visit It has been the practice at the Associated Medical Clinic of Philadelphia to have blood examination (red and white cells and hemoglobin) if the child is 10 per cent or more underweight or if he is noticeably pale

The advisability of performing the Wassermann test upon every child is an unsettled question * * * only about 2 per cent of children give a positive blood test * * * Many of these children have been so frightened by the abuse and so subdued by the hardships to which they have been subjected, that it seems certainly unwise, and possibly unkind to subject them to a Wassermann test for syphilis—or even a Pirquet test for tuberculosis infection—at the first visit as a necessary routine measure At this clinic it has been done * * * if the child shows clinical evidence of hereditary or acquired syphilis, if the child shows suspicious signs of hereditary or acquired syphilis, with foundlings, * * * if the child has suspicious sex history, or if his parents have undoubtedly been sexually promiscuous, or when there is a history of miscarriages

Certainly there can be no question as to the advisability of Schick testing for diphtheria at one of the first visits, and children reacting positively should be immunized with toxin-antitoxin before placement. Children not previously vaccinated should have this done, providing that they are to be placed under competent care

It is of great advantage to the examining clinic to be closely associated with a hospital In that case the opinion of consultants can easily be secured and X-ray examinations made, and if a child arrives at the clinic too ill to be sent to a foster home, he can be at once transferred to the hospital

Preferably all girls, and certainly those over 12 years of age, should be examined by a woman physician She should be a woman skilled not only in gynecological examinations but also in the psychology of girlhood * * *

The written record of this examination should be made in duplicate, one copy being kept in the office of the physician or the examining clinic and one sent at once to the agency referring the child. If possible, definite statements should be made as to the child's condition, and even more definite statements as to recommendations for the cure of defects * * * A definite time should be noted for the return of the child for subsequent examinations * * * As a general rule it is advisable to see any child who is 10 per cent or more underweight within from two to four weeks—or sooner if there is a suspicion of pulmonary tuberculosis.

Any child at all underweight or noticeably anemic should be seen by the physician every three months at least. Every child placed in a foster home should be completely reexamined at least once a year regardless of where he is. It is preferable that he return to the examining clinic for this purpose, so that the same person may examine and records may be more uniform This reexamination should be as thorough as the first examination

When the time comes for a child to leave the foster home and be discharged from the care of the society, he should again have a complete physical examination by the clinic or examining physician * * *. Any defects found even at this final examination should not be left unattended to, but definite arrangements should be made for him to have competent medical attention, either by a physician or at a hospital Especially is this true for children with chronic defects of such far-reaching importance as chronic heart or lung disease, rheumatism, nephritis, or congenital syphilis The last mentioned should be treated until the blood Wassermann becomes persistently negative[2]

Treatment.—Some plan should be worked out between the agency and one or more good hospitals whereby necessary tests, operations, and treatment can be obtained at a nominal or minimum cost In some cases the agency will be able to arrange with a hospital for laboratory tests; in other cases municipal or State service may be available. Where no free dental or eye clinics exist, a reliable dentist or eye specialist should be paid for this work on a yearly or per capita basis. Dental work especially is too often neglected by child-caring agencies

All treatment recommended should be secured as promptly as possible, except when some delay seems best from the standpoint of the child. With the control which can be exercised by an agency it should be possible to approach a 100-per cent correction of physical defects.

THE FOSTER MOTHER'S PART IN HEALTH

Restriction of the number of children in a foster home is one of the essentials to good health work on the part of the foster mother. Individual attention is the special need of many dependent children and of all babies. One or two older children are usually quite all that the foster home can absorb unless they are all members of one family With babies one child to a family is the ideal; two little children should be the limit The number of children placed in a foster home should also be governed by the number of own children of the foster parents.

Hygienic surroundings are imperative. These should include adequate sleeping space. Each child should have a bed to himself, and a room alone is still better The character of any person occupying the room with a child should be thoroughly known. All the hygienic requirements previously outlined for foster homes are necessary to health.

Foster family free from infectious disease—Doctor Jenks says: " The family physician should be consulted by the social worker, and it should be held no breach of professional secrecy for him to state at least in general terms whether the condition of either foster parent is such as to endanger the child."

The foster parents healthy and of cheerful disposition.—It is especially important for the welfare of the child that there should be freedom from nervous strain and friction in the home.

---

[2] Foster-Home Care for Dependent Children, pp. 114–115   U. S. Children's Bureau Publication No 136, Washington, 1929

Food must be ample, well cooked, properly balanced, adapted to the age of the child, and served at suitable hours. Growing boys and girls need plenty to eat; this is not luxury, but a necessity, and the agency must be willing to pay for it.

Rest.—Long hours of sleep with quiet and plenty of fresh air are needed by children. Great care must be taken to see that children are not overworked. Even conscientious foster parents sometimes do this without realizing it. Children who are underweight, restless, or anemic should have their hours of rest and play outlined in writing for the foster parents.

Oversight of recreation is difficult to secure but is very important, particularly for children who are in any sense problems. The foster parents should be interested enough to know where the children are at all times and in what way they amuse themselves. It is better still when they lead and guide their amusements.

Health habits.—The foster mother should be intelligent and firm in teaching health habits. She must be diligent in attending to such matters as the evacuation of bowels each morning and the cleaning of teeth. If the children have the habit of bed wetting,* she should withhold liquids in the evening and take the child to the toilet in the night. Her constant aim must be to get at the underlying causes of such habits. She must realize the need for regularity.

The care of the baby.—It is desirable, but not always possible, to have babies cared for in foster homes under the supervision of a trained nurse. Lacking this, they should be under close oversight of a good physician, and the foster mother must be well coached in the proper care of infants. There is so much good literature on the care and feeding of babies that there is no excuse for her being left in ignorance. The hygiene of the preschool child is also a matter on which she should be informed. (See Suggestions for further reading, p. 48.)

THE VISITOR'S PART IN HEALTH

The family health history.—The first task of the visitor in connection with the child's health begins with the original inquiry. The physician who examines the child should be supplied with a brief summary of the social history and home conditions and an accurate health history of the child and his family. The family history should cover the health of parents, grandparents, brothers, and sisters and should disclose the presence of tuberculosis, venereal disease, nervous disorders, mental diseases, and moral vagaries. The causes of deaths should be given. Special effort should be made to learn whether the child has been exposed to tuberculosis, venereal disease, or other infections from relatives or boarders in the home. Miscarriages and stillbirths have significance for the physician, and the birth dates of children may show whether the mother has suffered from too rapid childbearing.

The previous history of the child should be given, beginning with the mother's pregnancy, the birth and the child's condition, feeding during infancy, illness, contagious diseases of childhood, and later diseases, such as chorea, rheumatism, and tonsillitis. In cases of

---

* See Enuresis (separate from Child Management, U. S Children's Bureau Publication No. 143, Washington, 1928).

doubtful mentality any history of convulsions and the ages of walk-ing, talking, and entering school should be learned.

Carrying out the doctor's recommendations is the responsibility of the visitor when children are in boarding homes. Appointments for operations and visits to specialists and hospital clinics must be made by the visitor, and she must see that the child gets there, not once but many times, if necessary. In the free home, and especially in the case of children placed for adoption, medical care may well be the responsibility of the foster parents, but the visitor should advise when necessary and should see that nothing is neglected. In most foster homes, whatever their status, it is helpful for the visitor to interpret the medical findings to the foster parents, and she should see that the doctor's recommendations are carried out accurately. Every visit should be an occasion for definite inquiry as to health matters and such detailed instruction and advice to the foster mother as may seem needed.

Mental hygiene is a field which has been so hedged about with big words as to make simple things seem complicated. The essential facts are not new, however, but are largely matters of common sense. Many foster parents will have knowledge of a child's reactions and such a sympathetic understanding of his needs and desires that little help from the visitor will be needed. Others must be carefully taught how to train the child in good habits and advised as to which punishments are wise and which undesirable in their effects. The visitor should have enough theoretical knowledge of the subject to be of help. Here again there is printed material which will be of great assistance. Children who show marked peculiarities, whether of conduct, mental development, or habits, should be studied by a psychiatrist. In this connection a psychological test should precede and be a part of the report to the psychiatrist.

WANTED—A CHILD TO ADOPT

STOP, LOOK, AND LISTEN!

The finality of adoption.—Adoption is a legal process through which the child's natural parents or guardians waive all rights to him and the adopting parents assume the privileges and duties of own parents. Once the seal of the law is placed upon the relationship, legal responsibility is established. The child is severed for all time from those with whom he is connected by the closest of human ties. As this usually takes place before he has reached an age when he can have a voice in the matter, it follows that those responsible for his welfare can not use too much caution in making a decision so vital to his whole future

Adoption should never be planned in haste nor decided upon in an emergency. Ample time for consideration should be allowed the child's relatives and every possible assistance offered to enable them to rear him, before he is placed with a view to adoption. No tempo-rary or superficial situation should ever lead to the adoption of a child. No child should ever be separated from a parent because of poverty alone.

Some tests to apply:

1. If one or both parents are living, is it certain that, given the right kind of help, they can not care for the child now or at some future time?

2 If the reason for the separation is physical or mental disease of a parent, what about possible recovery? Also, may not permanent surrender of the child have a harmful effect on the parent?

3 If there is moral failure on the part of parents, have they been given every possible chance and incentive to improve? What will be the effect of depriving them of their child? Will the child suffer present harm from association with them? Does adoption represent an escape from responsibilities which could be discharged properly by the parents?

4 If the parents have abandoned the child, has an honest effort been made to trace them and learn the cause of desertion? Is it reasonably certain that they will not return to claim the child even after the provisions of the law have been complied with?

5. Is poverty the real reason for separation or abandonment?

6 If both parents are dead, is it certain that there are no relatives able and willing to give the child proper care?

7. Will adoption unnecessarily separate the child from brothers and sisters?

8. Is the child known to be physically and mentally fit for adoption?

Relatively few children will be found proper subjects for adoption, if their qualifications and the family circumstances are thus carefully considered.

THE ONLY SAFE WAY

A particularly searching inquiry should be made into the antecedents of the child to be adopted and of the foster family. This can not be overemphasized. When the child's parentage is known, the most exhaustive investigation should be made of the health and mentality of the parents, grandparents, uncles, aunts, brothers, and sisters. The circumstances of birth, the early influences to which the child was subjected, and every detail of his life that can be learned should be recorded, together with the history of the parents from their earliest childhood. All names and addresses of relatives should be obtained and kept, also what is learned as to their circumstances. The marriage record of the parents, birth record of the child, and any other papers identifying the child or containing valuable data should be carefully preserved.

Complete information as to their health and history should be furnished by the foster family which desires to take a child for all time. Refusal to do so should lead to rejection of the home. All the points outlined for any foster-home investigation should be covered with great thoroughness. In all cases the family physician should be seen. It is still more satisfactory, especially in cases where doubtful health conditions exist, to ask the foster parents to undergo a physical examination. In any case, the placing society should make sure that no tuberculosis, venereal disease, or mental or nervous instability exists in the family.

The financial ability of foster parents to raise a child and provide proper educational opportunities must be carefully considered. Even more important is the pliability of the family; that is, their ability to adapt themselves to the needs of children in general and especially to those of the child in question. In placing a young child for adoption, the capacity of the foster parents to care for the child as he then is must not be the only consideration. Their ability to carry him safely through later childhood and the critical age of adolescence must also be weighed.

In selecting an adoption home for a particular child, all the qualities of the foster home under consideration must be weighed against the needs of the child available for adoption. His physical needs are easily determined with the aid of good medical service. His mental and spiritual requirements are difficult enough to foresee, even with the fullest information about him. All that is known as to his personality should be supplemented by the completest possible picture of his background, and by studies of his mentality and temperament made by competent persons. No child should be placed for adoption in this day without being tested mentally, even when this involves considerable trouble and expense. Tests have been devised for children as young as 6 months of age. These tests, if repeated every three to six months, give a fairly accurate index of the mentality of children

The material, cultural, and spiritual gifts offered by the foster home must be nicely balanced against one another and against the capacities and gifts of the child. The reasons of the foster parents for wishing to take a child are extremely important. They must want the child not as a plaything or a cause for pride, nor merely as an outlet for thwarted emotions.

The attitude of relatives of the foster parents toward the proposed adoption should be favorable. The child should meet with a welcome from foster grandparents, aunts, and uncles and, above all, from foster brothers and sisters

It should be obvious that if this discrimination enters into the selection of adoption homes, the barbarous practice of lining up a group of children and allowing prospective foster parents to " take their pick " will be relegated to the limbo of the outgrown past.

Children with bad or unknown heritage should rarely be placed for adoption, and then only after the strictest precautions are observed. If cases of insanity, epilepsy, feeble-mindedness, or syphilis exist among the child's forbears, the only safe plan is to keep the child in a boarding home under observation for a period of two or three years, meantime giving him every known physical and mental test. Foundlings and children about whose father nothing is known should be treated in the same way.

Some years ago a reputable children's society placed two infants of unknown but different parentage in a cultured family of ample means. Every test known to science was given at the time of placement, the results seemed satisfactory, and the adoption went through. To-day one of those children is in an institution for the feeble-minded. The other, a girl of 11, is under treatment for hereditary syphilis, with every chance of becoming a hopeless cripple. Thousands of dollars and a wealth of affection and care have been expended by these unfortunate foster parents with this heartbreaking result.

If children with diseased or degenerate ancestry are finally, after prolonged observation, pronounced normal and placed for adoption, the foster parents should be fully informed of the risk involved.

Full information about any child placed for adoption should be given the foster parents at the time the child is first placed or as soon thereafter as adoption is contemplated. In some cases the facts need not be given in too stark detail, but the main facts should be known. The foster parents who do not want to know anything about the child they adopt are risking much through their ignorance. It is their duty as well as their right to know as much as possible about the child whom they are to nurture and direct.

A written agreement had best be made with the foster parents at the time of placement. There should be at least a letter, stating clearly the terms of placement and the control to be exercised by the agency, a copy of which is kept on file. The foster family should understand that the agreement can be revoked by either party at any time until the legal adoption takes place

At least one year of trial residence in the adoption home under supervision of the placing society should precede the completion of adoption proceedings, whether this is required by law or not. If at the end of that period there seems to be any doubt that the child will do well in a home, a longer trial is advisable. This period is the visitor's great opportunity, and her only one, to prepare the adopting parents for their task and to observe how they perform it. Her work should be delicate and thorough, calling forth all that she has to give.

Reinvestigation before adoption should always be made This should cover—

1. The present situation in the child's own family. Could they possibly care for the child now, and if so, would it be detrimental to the child to return to them?

2. Any changes in the household of the foster family and their possible effect upon the welfare and status of the child.

3. The opinion of a few carefully selected references as to the success of the placement.

4. The child's own attitude toward adoption, if he is old enough to be consulted.

5. The effect of adoption upon the child's status with the family and community. This is sometimes a strong argument in favor of an adoption which might otherwise seem inadvisable. A child who is legally one of the family often has a different feeling and stands better in the eyes of those about him than one who is regarded as a mere beneficiary.

6. A thorough mental and physical examination of the child. A mental examination is imperative in adoption cases, even though considerable expense and trouble are involved. This should be made at the time of first placement. A reexamination is desirable at the time of adoption as a check on the first examination.

7. A review by more than one person of the whole record of the child's progress since placement. In making the final decision the visitor should always be aided by other members of the staff or board of managers.

Informing the child of adoption—Foster parents should always explain to the child that he has been adopted If children adopted when very young are kept in ignorance that they are not own children, they almost invariably learn of it later, and this is sometimes a serious shock.   On the other hand, if the thought is perfectly familiar from earliest childhood, it does not in any way affect their feeling for their foster parents and is a protection   The information can be presented by the foster parents in such a way as to increase rather than destroy a child's love for them and confidence in them. One little girl who was adopted with her baby brother was heard to remark proudly to her little cousins by adoption, " You're *own* children, but we're *chosen* children."

ENDING SUPERVISION

After adoption actually takes place, the whole responsibility for the child passes to the foster parents.   Supervision should definitely cease, the visitor entering the home, if at all, like any invited guest.   If she has been successful in her work, invitations will not be lacking, but she should not make her visits an occasion for unsolicited advice. The whole aim of supervision should be to lead up to the point where advice will be unnecessary and the foster parents will be independent of the society.   It is highly desirable, however, that the feeling of the foster family be such that they will naturally keep the representatives of the society informed of the progress of the child   Such information should be carefully recorded, as it is a valuable index to the soundness of the work being done

PLACEMENT BY THE INSTITUTION

Nearly 25 years ago (January, 1909) the famous White House Conference on the Care of Dependent Children was convened by President Roosevelt.   About 200 people representing every phase of child welfare, including institutional care, were present   In the conclusions unanimously adopted by this group was the following:

Home life is the highest and finest product of civilization * * *   Children should not be deprived of it except for urgent and compelling reasons.   Except in unusual circumstances the home should not be broken up for reasons of poverty   The carefully selected foster home is for the normal child the best substitute for the natural home   For the temporary or more or less permanent care of children different methods are in use, notably the plan of placing them in families, paying for their board, and the plan of institutional care   Unless and until such homes are found, the use of institutions is necessary

Since that conference there has been a growing realization on the part of those connected with institutional work that most children thrive better in private homes, and there has been a marked extension of the activities of institutions into the field of foster-family care. In all parts of the country agencies may now be found giving both types of care.   A few institutions have even gone so far as to close their doors and devote their energies entirely to the care of children in foster homes.   Other institutions have used placement for children in particular need of individual care and attention, such as those presenting special health or conduct difficulties, developing a few carefully selected homes into practically an extension of the institution

Institutions have always done more or less placement. The necessity of making some plan for children too old to remain longer in the institution, the pressure from new applicants for space, and the difficulty of coping with certain types of children in a group have led many institutions to make use of free or wage homes, and less frequently of boarding homes. Too often such placement has been done only with the fringes of attention, so to speak, with no clear realization of the difficulties or the far-reaching consequences. It has been done casually, by busy executive, by trustees, or by almost anyone who was interested and thought he knew of a " good home." The results of such placements have been deplorable, both for the children concerned and because of their influence on the attitude of parents, the public, and institutional authorities.

The prejudice which exists against foster-family care on the part of many people is largely the direct result of careless or ignorant methods of placement on the part of both institutions and child-placing agencies This poor work is characterized by—

Failure to learn enough about children upon reception or to record what has been learned.

Needless breaking up of families.

Needless separation of children of the same family.

Failure to make proper investigation of homes in which children are to be placed.

Too low standards for foster homes

Unskilled choice of homes for particular children.

Lack of attention to health of both foster family and children.

Lack of good supervision of children placed in foster families, with consequent failure to guard them from abuse, neglect, and overwork.

The way for institutions to make placements is to follow the same principles laid down for other foster-care agencies, both in receiving children into care and in sending them to foster-family homes. This is more easily said than done. All child-caring institutions should have the services of a properly qualified social worker to investigate applications for care and to place and supervise outgoing children. Those institutions which find employment of a full-time case worker impractical should draft any trained person in sight to make their inquiries. Better still, when children are to be discharged, instead of being placed in any family that happens to be available, by a busy institution superintendent who will have no time to supervise, they should be transferred to the care of a children's aid society or some other agency whose business it is to care for children in foster families

The institution which can not afford a social worker and has no child-placing agency to which it can turn must face the fact that it can not hope to do satisfactory work until a solution is found If it will first turn its attention to the careful sifting of applications, it will soon reduce the number of children received for care and thus free funds and energy for better work with those ready for discharge

An outlet for critics.—Critics who think it the duty of a children's agency to take in every child brought to its doors, "and no questions asked," may well be urged to turn their attention to the strengthening of community resources looking to the preservation of the homes which will be broken up if all the children for whom application is made are accepted.

THIS QUESTION OF RECORDS

WHY RECORDS ARE NEEDED

In justice to the child, the facts and proofs of his origin should be scrupulously preserved for the protection of his legal and social rights and for his satisfaction in later life. Lack of a birth record may cause endless trouble. No proof of parentage may mean a lost inheritance. It sometimes happens that for a time a children's agency is the only link between different members of a family. Failure to keep information has frequently led to the various members of a household being lost to one another for all time. The individual thus left stranded in society with no known connections is apt to feel more or less of a social outcast He is invariably tormented by a longing to know about his people.

An adult has the right to know all about himself; certainly no person should presume to withhold the information from him. To learn the truth after the age of full understanding has been reached is sometimes a serious shock. It is better for every child to grow up familiar with the main facts of his history. He need not be given every unpleasant detail, but neither should he be told anything untrue. Children who learn by chance that they have been deceived may lose confidence in those around them and become suspicious of everyone.

A change of visitors is a catastrophe to an agency which has not good records. Valuable information may be irretrievably lost. Both child and foster family will suffer from lack of understanding and from a change of methods which may be quite unintentional. The new visitor is sure to duplicate and waste much effort before she grasps the details of the situation. The fuller the records the less the break will matter

From the standpoint of convenience, dependence on memory for facts. dates, and action taken in connection with the care of a child leads to endless confusion and embarrassment and sometimes to legal complications If a difference arises with the child's parents or with the foster mother; if any agency asks for information; if there is a court hearing—in fact at every turn, the visitor who does not keep full records is forced to appear inaccurate and unbusinesslike

To work out a coherent plan over any period without a record of the information upon which it is based and of all important steps and developments is impossible. To proceed without a record is like entering a labyrinth without the clue. To leave out important links is to allow the clue to be broken.

The only way to measure the past—or for that matter the present—work of a social agency is through a study of its records If intelligently kept, records may be the source of valuable social data.

WHAT RECORDS MUST BE KEPT[4]

In planning a record system one must have an eye to the future. Lack of time and of stenographic service may preclude the possibility of ideally full records for the time being, but the framework should be provided so that as conditions improve no radical changes will be needed. Large agencies may add many other conveniences, but the following is such a framework, suitable for child-placing agencies and for institutions of any size:

1. CARD INDEXES

A card index, filed alphabetically, should include all families which apply for care, not merely those whose children are accepted A separate index should be used for foster homes. Cards 3 by 5 inches in size will be satisfactory for these indexes.

The family is the best unit for indexing and numbering for these purposes. At the top of the card the surname should be followed by the names of both parents and the maiden name of the mother, a complete list of the children with dates of birth appearing below. The date of application, the address, and the case number complete the identifying information. Cases of remarriage should be indicated and cross indexed. It is helpful to check or underline the names of children taken into care.

A third card index based on children will be found very helpful for compiling a monthly report of agency activities. The file should be divided into sections representing the status of each case; that is, applications pending; children in institutions; children in foster homes; and children under supervision elsewhere. Each of these sections may be further divided to show whether applications or cases have been carried over from a preceding month or have been closed and whether cases are new, old, or reopened. If a card for each child is filed according to these classifications, compiling material for a monthly statement of volume of service takes but a short time.

2. A CHRONOLOGICAL RECORD OF ADMISSIONS AND DISCHARGES

The chronological record of admissions and discharges should show the names of all children received for care, with dates of admission and discharge, and enough other information to identify the child It may be kept on sheets of ledger size for insertion in a permanent record.

3. A FILE OF FAMILY FOLDERS

The file of family folders should be of manila cardboard, letter size (8½ by 11 inches), and should be kept, if possible, in a steel filing cabinet which will lock and will be reasonably fireproof. The practice of using a separate folder for each child in care is confusing and carries the danger of loss of identity or relationship. The habit of viewing the child as a member of a family is a good one to cultivate even here.

Filing the folders in alphabetical order is most practical for small or new agencies, but they should be numbered in the order in which

---

[4] Sample record forms may be obtained from the Child Welfare League of America, 130 East Twenty-second Street, New York, N Y

the families come under care. This is with an eye to the future, as larger agencies usually file by number. Histories in active use should be filed alphabetically and in a separate place for ready reference. The family record should consist of—

A face sheet.—Many children's agencies use for the entire family one face sheet similar to that in use by most family welfare associations. Other agencies prefer an individual face sheet for each child under care, which contains a certain amount of information about the family. This information should be completely filled in for each child, not merely for the oldest or the first child received for care.

The findings of the initial inquiry.—These are sometimes summarized on a page of the face sheet, or they may be entered on a card of the same size as the face sheet. This summary represents the very minimum that should be known about a child before he is taken. If possible, it should be amplified to include a record of every visit made in the course of the inquiry and the information obtained. Additional information should be recorded as secured.

A record of placements with dates of admission and discharge is sometimes provided for on a page of the face sheet, or it may be kept on a separate card of the same size as the face sheet. This record should be accurate and kept up to date so that it will show at all times just where the child is. It should never be destroyed even after the child's discharge.

A chronological history of supervision.—A separate record of supervision must be kept for each child in a family unless they are placed together. To avoid the repetition of information pertaining to the family rather than to any particular child, it may be added to the initial inquiry under the proper dates, instead of to each child's record. All this should be typed if possible.

A record of physical and mental examinations.—Records of all physical, psychological, or psychiatric examinations should be kept. Every case record should include at least a report of the physical examination made when the child was accepted for care.

Correspondence.—Since much of the correspondence may concern several of the children of a family it is most convenient to keep it clipped together in the order received. References to letters concerning each child should be entered under the proper dates on each child's history. All important letters should be kept, but it saves time in the end to give the gist of a letter in the history.

Important papers, such as legal documents and birth records, may be placed in envelopes and labeled before being filed in the family folder. This is a good method of treating any very confidential information.

4. THE FOSTER-HOME RECORD

The record of foster homes, together with correspondence relating to the home, should be kept in its own folder and in a separate place from the records of children. It should consist of—

A face sheet giving a picture of the make-up of the family with such facts as ages, nationality, religion, occupation. It should give the address with directions for reaching the home and facts about the home such as the number of rooms, existence of yard, conveniences, location with reference to transportation, neighbors, school, and church.

A record of the inquiry, preferably arranged chronologically, should cover all interviews, with name, position of person seen, and information gained. Brief descriptions of references are necessary to give an idea of the value of their opinions. In describing a visit to the home it may be helpful to use the headings on page 18.

Subsequent entries after a home is in use, summing up from time to time its weaknesses and good points, are very much worth while Any important changes in the household should be entered. If use of the home is discontinued the reason should be given on this record and should also be entered on the foster-home face sheet.

A record of children placed in a home should be kept with dates of placement and discharge and reason for leaving. This may be kept on the back of the foster-home face sheet or on a separate card of the same size. This will show at a glance how many and what children are in any home at a given time and how many the home has cared for altogether. With boarding homes the amount due for board monthly may be calculated in a few minutes from these cards, and also the number of days' care given. It is important to enter the ages of the children.

In The Work of Child-placing Agencies (U. S. Children's Bureau Publication No. 171, p. 83) the following description is given of the records of a children's society: "These followed a well-developed outline and gave in each case such a clear picture of the home itself as well as of the character, education, and background of the foster parents, that the reader felt as if he really knew what manner of people the applicants were and what kind of a child would be likely to fit into their home."

RECORDS ARE CONFIDENTIAL

Not only should the records themselves be guarded from improper use, but the persons familiar with their contents should regard them as sacred. This applies as much to the confidences of children as to those of adults, and what is learned from references as well as from the people concerned.

This does not mean, however, that practically all the information on file should not be available to responsible representatives of other social agencies. Without such interchange of information there can be no true working together for the welfare of the children concerned. Files should also be opened freely for impersonal study and research by accredited persons.

When stories are used for publicity purposes, names, addresses, and identifying information should never be divulged.

AFTER DISCHARGE—WHAT?
WHILE THE CHILD IS AWAY FROM HIS FAMILY

Preparing the home for the child's return.—It is a mistake to assume that all children for whom foster care is asked are from bad homes. As the kind of care and the expertness of the service offered by child-placing agencies improve, parents of a higher type turn to the agencies for aid. Some are able to pay all expenses. Many are quite competent to judge what is best for their children. Poor people may be cultured and uneducated people intelligent. The finest moral qualities may be associated with dire misfortune. A request for help may imply self-sacrifice and forethought rather than incapacity. An entire absence of condescension and an open mind are the first requisites in dealing with parents.

It goes without saying that there is some lack or dislocation in the home which must give up its children. It is the plain duty of any agency which receives children for care to see that everything possible is done to adjust the difficulties which have led to a child's removal from his rightful home, if the elements of such home still exist. In some cases it may be possible to leave or delegate this work of adjustment to a family agency, a health agency, the courts, or some other agency. If not, the children's society must accept this responsibility for its wards, otherwise it is only half doing its job.

Every resource should be exhausted in an effort to meet such needs as medical care, financial help, and employment. If the parents are ignorant or irresponsible, the harder task of improving living standards must be attempted. No spectacular or sudden reforms need be looked for. Re-education of adults is at best a slow and painful process, and the visitor will be unable to affect such fundamentals as intellectual endowment and industrial ability. She can, in most cases, hope to quicken in the parents such a sense of responsibility for the support, health, education, moral well-being, and happiness of the child as will help to make the home a better place for him upon his return. The visitor who is equipped to do so may assist educated as well as uninformed parents to understand and meet the peculiar problems of children who present health or conduct difficulties. In this she may be helped by the wave of *parent education* that is sweeping the country. The basis for success in the work of building up better homes is practical knowledge of social conditions and of the way people are molded by them, combined with genuine friendliness and tolerance.

Preparing the child to go home.—If a child may sometime go back to his own people, it is vital that he should never lose touch with them. It is possible for the affection between parents and child to be strengthened by a limited separation, if it be made an opportunity to bring out a devotion which has been taken too much for granted.

Parents should never be criticized, even in the presence of a very young child. This does not mean that an attempt should be made to hide what is certainly known. No deceit should be used. A child should not be made to feel blame when his parents are the real culprits, but older children can be given an insight into their parents' struggles and hardships. Their good qualities and their need for the child's affection and help can be stressed. The child's loyalty, his desire to be of use, his protective instinct may be appealed to.

No training given a child in health habits, good manners, and conduct will be quite lost when he returns home, even though he has been a reluctant subject. He may even improve when he gets home, doing better when thrown on his own responsibility. He may also pass on what he has learned to other children in the family and even to his elders.

How the foster family can help.—The aid of the foster family should be enlisted in keeping home ties vital and wholesome Jealousy on the part of the child's own parents can not always be avoided, but the foster parent who knowingly causes it or tries to wean a child from his own people is not the one for the job. Unless all contact with the child's own parents is to be broken off, it is undesirable for the child to apply the terms "mother" and "father" to the foster parents. "Uncle" and "aunt" will not arouse antagonism and will suggest the proper relationship.

Before a child whose relatives are to visit him is placed, the foster parents should be told what to expect and prepare to welcome them. On the other hand, parents should be warned of the harm to the child of interference or of rousing his dissatisfaction. They should be asked to bring any complaints to the visitor.

The influence on parents of visits to a good foster home where they are made welcome is often more effective than anything the visitor can say or do They absorb valuable object lessons in ways of living, methods of discipline, health matters, and ideals of conduct, and these lessons are the more effective through being unintended If the foster parents have won the child, the very eagerness of the parents to retain his respect and affection for themselves will stimulate them to imitation.

Working with other agencies.—If, while the child is under care, the home is under the supervision of some other agency besides the children's society, it is of the utmost importance that the two organizations keep in close touch and work in harmony. In this connection an occasional conference should be held to discuss the situation in the home and the progress of the child, with a view to his return.

WHEN THE CHILD GOES HOME

Investigation for the child's return.—Before any child whose home conditions are at all questionable is allowed to go home, an inquiry as to the present conditions in the home is in order. This should cover much the same ground as that made in choosing a foster home; but, if the parents have the proper attitude, lower standards must sometimes be accepted as possible in a child's own home than in a foster home. If the home has been under the supervision of some other agency during the child's absence, both this survey of home conditions and the aftercare of the child may be delegated to this agency, always presupposing close cooperation. More often it will be necessary for the society caring for the child to assume responsibility for his return home.

After temporary care, such as that given during a short illness of the mother, it will be necessary only to see that the conditions which made removal of the child imperative are thoroughly cleared up— that the mother is able to care for her family, for instance. Even after a long period of care such as might be necessitated by sanitarium treatment for the mother, if the family is intelligent, there is no serious poverty, and the medical supervision is good, the children's agency may safely drop out.

After prolonged care.—When an agency has cared for a child over a period of years, it is morally bound to make sure that no harm results from that child's discharge. No one has the right to take a girl from unfavorable surroundings, protect and train her for years, and then allow her, at the critical age of 16 or 18, to drift back to a family that has ceased to feel responsible for her and to face dangers for which she is totally unprepared. Even when children are younger or home conditions are good, the loss of the friendships and associations built up through the foster home, the process of renewing old ties, and the making of new ones are hard for most of them. The closest supervision sometimes is needed to tide children over these experiences to a period of stability.

Children entering employment —The child who has no home and who has not been legally adopted must remain a charge on the agency until he becomes self-supporting If funds are low the agency may be tempted to let him leave school as soon as the law allows, especially if he has the usual adolescent eagerness to get to work. This is a shortsighted policy. It is to the interest of society that every child receive all the education he can profit by For some this will mean merely finishing grammar school, for others high school, for still others it will call for college training Many will need a trade training which is not now available in many places but which should be diligently sought. Exceptional gifts, as in music or art, warrant special training.

If the foregoing policy has been followed, agency wards who are ready to become self-supporting should have some choice when they begin work Left to themselves, however, young people are apt to take the first position open, paying little attention to whether it is work for which they are fitted, or whether it promises advancement. They think of wages, but hours and working conditions mean little to them as yet. Here the most careful and experienced guidance is needed.

The records of the agency should afford material for study of each child's aptitudes which will be valuable in steering him into the right vocation. The mental test that should have been given to the exceptionally gifted child as well as the unusually dull one will help in guidance The child's own opinions and desires should be checked against his limitations and abilities Other things being equal, he is most likely to succeed in the job he picks for himself, but he can be steered in his choice.

Nothing should be too much trouble at this time Next to the period of infancy, that of adolescence and the beginning of work life is the most crucial. The child who must make his way without the backing of a family is under a great handicap. The least an agency can do for him is to smooth the way to a happy and successful vocation and help him to find the right social setting.

The choice of a boarding place for the boy or girl with no family may decide the trend of a life. If the surroundings are sordid or degrading, if opportunities for social life and wholesome companionship are lacking, failure or even tragedy may result It is no easy task to find favorable social opportunities for the boy or girl who has no home ties. It may prove still more difficult to persuade the child to accept them at the moment when he first feels the thrill of independence. Here the visitor who has won a child's confidence finds her reward and her chance to clinch all that has gone before.

IN CONCLUSION

Man is a social being. He springs from the soil of family life, from it he draws sustenance, to it he is bound by innumerable fibers. When for any reason he is uprooted, his well-being demands that he be transplanted and nurtured with the same tender solicitude for conditions of atmosphere, soil, and sun that the careful gardener displays toward his seedlings From infancy through adolescence the fundamental need of a human being is the opportunity for undisturbed growth. A child should be deeply rooted; bound to his environment on every side by ties of interest, habit, and affection. Only so can he attain the stability to withstand the storms of later life and make his fullest contribution to society.

SUGGESTIONS FOR FURTHER READING

1935. Books and Pamphlets for Parents. Children's Bureau, U S Department of Labor, Washington Mimeographed 18 pp Free

A selected list of books on the care and training of children

1934. Child Training; a manual for foster parents, by Jessie A Charters. State Department of Public Welfare, Division of Charities, Columbus, Ohio 126 pp 30 cents

A booklet that has been tried out experimentally with a large group of foster parents It deals directly with the problems they meet and is arranged in convenient form for use in study groups

1933. A Good Foster Home; its achievements and limitations, by Carl R. Rogers. Mental Hygiene (published by the National Committee for Mental Hygiene, 450 Seventh Avenue, New York), vol 17, no 1 (January), pp. 21–40 Available in most libraries.

A discussion of a home in which 10 small boys, previously maladjusted, made unmistakable improvement

Standards for Children's Organizations Providing Foster Family Care. Child Welfare League of America (130 East Twenty-second Street, New York) 24 pp 20 cents

Standards derived from the experience of organizations that are members of the Child Welfare League of America and used by the League in passing on eligibility for membership

1932. Foster Mothers: Successful and Unsuccessful; based on cases described by Virginia Dudley Smith College Studies in Social Work (Northampton Mass), vol 3, no 2 (December), pp 151–182 75 cents

A critical study of 22 foster homes in use in October 1929 by the New England Home for Little Wanderers A limited number of copies of this issue of the studies are available

1921. The Child in the Foster Home, by Sophie Van Senden Theis and Constance Goodrich. New York School of Social Work 150 pp 75 cents For sale at The Bookshop, Family Welfare Association of America, 130 East Twenty-second Street, New York, N Y

An account of the experiences of the Child Placing Agency of the New York State Charities Aid Association in the placement and supervision of children in free foster homes

48

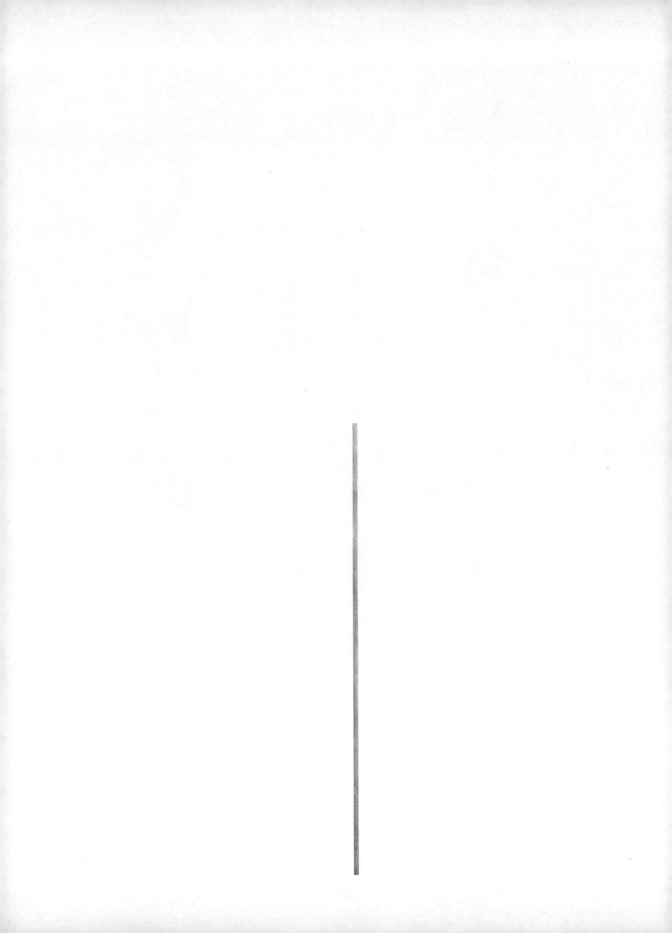

Lightning Source UK Ltd.
Milton Keynes UK
UKOW02f2214070114

224182UK00007B/411/P